Real Estate Investing

Roadmap to Wealth

Real Estate Investing

ROADMAP TO WEALTH

CHARLIE EINSMANN • SAM JACKNIN • ED GRASS

Roadmap to Wealth: Real Estate Investing
By Charlie Einsmann, Sam Jacknin, Ed Grass

First Edition

Published by
Munn Avenue Press
300 Main Street, Ste 21
Madison, NJ 07940
MunnAvenuePress.com

MUNN AVENUE PRESS

Paperback ISBN# 978-1-960299-24-6
Printed in the United States of America

TABLE OF CONTENTS

PART 3

PART 4

INTRODUCTION

Should You Really Buy This Book?

Sam, Ed, and I wrote this book after developing our own very successful careers in real estate investing. We wrote it to supply you with a concrete guide to turning your desire, commitment, and hard work into wealth. We will teach you how to effectively create and deploy capital – even if you start with next to none – to generate equity and a passive income stream through residential real estate investing.

What does this mean? It means this is not a get-rich-*quick* book – it is a *get-rich* book. If you want schemes and secrets that will show you how to get real estate leads and deals to fall from the sky into your lap (or for a 'small' fee), buy another book or get an internet club membership for entertainment value. To be honest, as we will be throughout this book, lottery tickets would probably be a better use of your money than those options. Frankly, we wrote this book, in part, out of disgust watching people get fleeced out of big money by grifters who talk about real estate investing but never really lived it. Worse, they have no idea how to help you take concrete, realistic, and effective action.

In these pages, for the price of a book, we distill our experience into a roadmap to explain *exactly* what *you* need to do so *you* can make money (and not for us to make money off of you). If you want to know the realistic and achievable steps to understand, find, and execute profitably on residential real estate purchases, rentals, sales, borrowing, lending, and more, then this is the book for you. You will learn everything you need to succeed.

We identified and followed these steps to create our real estate wealth through twenty years of trial and error. We can and will show you precisely what to do and how to do it, whether you have $100,000 in the bank or $10,000, or even just $1,000. If you are starting on second base with significant capital, great, we will tell you how to start from there as well.

Hang in there and be prepared to learn and work. This book will help you reach your goals sooner than we did and more effectively and rapidly than you might think possible. Others already have successfully followed our path to real estate success, so why not you? Fortify your courage and drive, and then use this roadmap to go from surviving to thriving with real estate holdings generating a comfortable income stream for you.

Part 1

THE BIG PICTURE

"If I am right about the big picture, I will be rewarded for my patience." —Thomas Kaplan

"A lot of times we base everything just on our immediate circumstances. We don't see a big picture for our lives." —Jennifer Holiday

"Having the big picture in mind enables us to overcome the day-to-day routines that attempt to distract us from pursuing our dreams." —Assegid Habtewood

Chapter 1

OVERVIEW OF THE PATHWAY

"There is no elevator to success you must take the stairs."
—Zig Ziglar

Most great compositions start with an overture. Think of musical theater or an orchestra. The overture acts as an introduction to the entire work and focuses the attentive listener on important themes they will hear repeated throughout. The overture serves as a musical outline of what is to come so you can follow the story and not miss or fail to connect important plot points. With this in mind, chapter one of this book will act as our overture to success in real estate investing. The following sections will then introduce who we are, how we work, the way we have developed and grown our business, and some of the key stepping stones you should follow along the way.

This chapter offers a bird's eye view of what is to come before we start digging deep into detail. Even if you are itching to get a move-on and decide to skip to chapter two, this chapter will be waiting for you when you need a digestible recap from time to time. In this chapter, we also include a lot of details you will use throughout the book to help you succeed, but we don't want you to get lost in the weeds. So at least bookmark this page as a place to return to focus on the big themes and big picture that are essential if you want to make good decisions as you journey through real estate investing.

. . .

The Birth of the Model

First of all, let me introduce our real estate investing trio and your authors. I'm Charlie Einsmann, also known as "The Maverick," "Rain Man" or as Tim Grover ("Relentless") would say "The Cleaner." My background is in engineering, and data, not taking "no" for an answer, and just getting things done!

I met Sam Jacknin ("The Broker") in 2000 when he was a client services manager and director while we were both working for an internet company in Herndon, Virginia. Sam is our business guy, the member of the trio who holds an MBA. We were both doing well in our respective positions but shared a dream to leave cubicle hell and be our own bosses. If this is your dream, keep reading, we may be onto something and you don't want to miss out!

We brainstormed around the proverbial water cooler and came to the conclusion that investing in real estate could be the key to unlocking our corporate straightjackets. No, this isn't an original idea, but that doesn't make it a bad one. We also thought it would be a relatively low-risk operation. Of course, there is always risk attached to big career moves, but we were positive thinkers. Surely, this decision would be "as safe as houses" that are tangible! And, we thought, doesn't everybody need a place to live? Sam had already obtained a real estate license a few years earlier to keep his options open and fill the wall space next to his MBA. Therefore, he was the first to take the bull by the horns and move into real estate full-time in 2001 – a new life for a new millennium. I was a little behind and eased into part-time real estate in 2003.

Sam first met Ed Grass while he was still a partner at a big law firm. Starting as friends hanging out at their kids' bus stop, Ed later invested with me and Sam in a project called Clear Sky Car Wash, which was a very early iteration of our company and grand scheme to create passive income streams. You see, before creating our real estate pathway we tried to build and own a car wash. Unfortunately, this first big project together would not go as smoothly as we would have liked. Not long after opening, our car wash was seized by eminent domain to be bull-dozed by the government for use as a highway on-ramp! How about that for an unexpected business problem? The government offered us far less than its value, especially given the decades of functional life and easy income stream we had created but would never enjoy. Worse, they only offered about the same amount of money we owed our investors and banks for normal start-up loans. We would have walked away with just about nothing in return for years' worth of sweat and blood to obtain the land, learn about car wash operations, find a contractor, and build this valuable income-producing asset.

Ed jumped in to lead our legal fight for three years. We ultimately recovered the true value of our investment, almost unheard of in such disputes. We then used everything gained after paying off investors and banks as seed money for our new three-person real estate holding company which started with zero real estate! We quickly learned it was going to take hard work and determination to overcome inevitable (if sometimes unpredictable) problems and succeed at this real estate thing.

By 2005, Sam and I were working together full-time in real estate, with Ed adding his creative ideas and detailed analysis to the group effort. Pretty soon, we had formed our very own underground real estate lair. Here we set about building our roadmap and plotting our path. They say that nothing worth doing comes easy, and this was certainly true for us. It took us years of hard work, learning, and a lot of trial and error before we ended up developing a realistic residential investing strategy. But those years of stress and uncertainty were totally worth it. Our faith, determination, and patience paid off. To put it bluntly, we developed a model that has made us millions and now we get to write a book about it.

During this process, we first realized that our model was repeatable when it started working for our friends and associates who followed along on our path behind us. This means there's plenty of proof that our roadmap can work for you too. To be clear, this was not luck. We devised a strategy that works reliably and can be taught to others, which are key steps to validate any theory. This book not only provides you with details of our model for success but also signposts the highs and lows of our journey, so hopefully you can swerve around some of the potholes we didn't see until we hit them on our way.

It is through pride, rather than a lack of modesty, that I tell you this: We have created the ultimate residential real estate investing ecosystem. This model can be applied to specific regions or nationwide. While it hasn't been tested internationally, most of the concepts should work with the right tweaks to fit local laws and real estate markets. What makes our book different is that we already have money. We are not trying to get rich off of you, like so many shysters out there who sell fantasy leads and get-rich schemes. Instead, we are delighted that we can share our success with you by showing you the right ingredients to mix with your hard work to reach your goals.

Our Roadmap Model

We will begin by outlining, on a macro level, how you can start with very little and grow a business that provides you with a generous residual income. We will teach you how to make your first profit through residential investing. Then we will explain how you can convert some of that initial lump sum into residual income, meaning cash-producing assets, to generate more in residual income than you initially invested in assets over time.

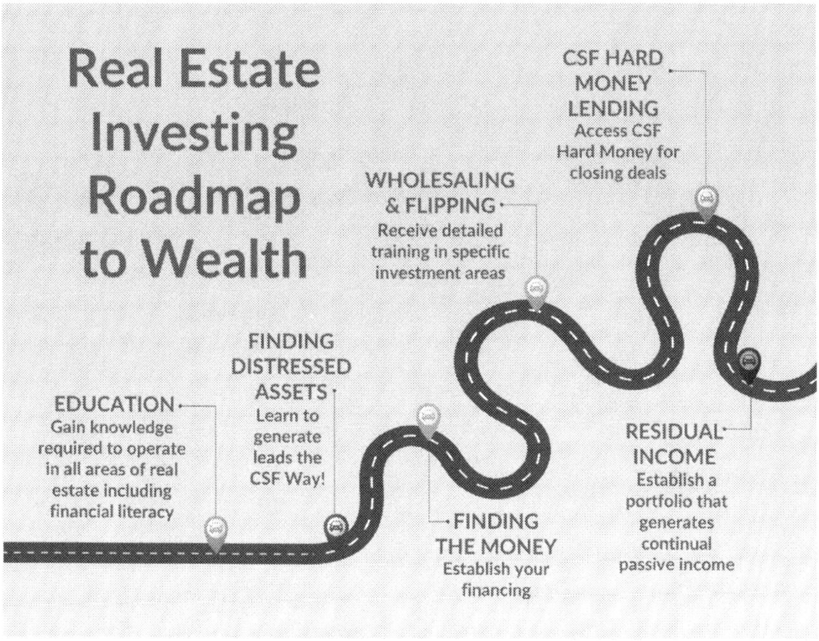

You will hear a lot about team building in this book. Despite being in this game for over twenty years, none of us, as individuals, possess all the skills that are required to succeed in real estate investing. Teamwork really does make the dream work. Corny, yes, but a true key to success is to build a team of talent; with every member offering a valuable ingredient to the pot. We would not have found the land for the carwash without Charlie, nor put together the capital and deal without Sam, nor overcome the government without Ed. Together, we won and kept winning.

Everything we share with you is designed to inspire you and never deter you. There are, of course, challenges along the way, but with solid advice, a sound strategy, and belief in yourself, you can follow in our footsteps and reap the rewards. Of course, you cannot build your dream team overnight. While not a requirement, recall how Sam, Ed, and I all first met and got to know each other well as friends and colleagues. You will cause more harm than good if you swing for the fences immediately on adding partners or making deals. Instead, let ours be a model that you can reference both in the short- and long-term as you get up to speed and then hit the gas. Ask yourself where your education and skills can play a part, and then identify which gaps you would need to fill to have a fully functional team. We tell you below how to make this happen.

More about our team: We call ourselves The Maverick, The Broker, and The Lawyer. None of us are fighter pilots, incidentally, we will leave that to Tom Cruise. I, Charlie Einsmann, aka The Maverick, love talking to anyone with the hope of finding a deal almost anywhere but, admittedly, I very occasionally get us into trouble because I am action-oriented. Sam Jacknin, aka The Broker, documents and manages the deals through to the conclusion and tries to keep us out of the above-mentioned trouble by attending to daily details. And finally, Ed, aka The Lawyer, and most cautious of us, gets our team out of trouble when the Broker fails to control my Maverick tendencies! I've even grown to the point where I run things by Ed in advance if I see any potential storm clouds.

Of course, I am over-generalizing just a little. The most important thing is that we all respect and trust each other and recognize that our greatness is dependent on the sum of all three parts. We all enjoy learning from each other, analyzing possible deals, and thinking creatively. Along the way, I've learned a good bit of the law (thanks to Ed and Rick Oppenheim, Jr.) and I have developed a great eye for bird-dogging deals. Sam has managed all the assets while creating an efficient backend allowing us to expand with less. Ed not only has learned about real estate deal-making but will even talk nicely to some people some of the time!

Fast-forwarding to today from my computer career knowing little about real estate, I am now co-founder of Clear Sky Financial LLC (CSF), a hard money lender in DC, Maryland, Virginia, North Carolina, and Florida. I am also co-founder of Clear Sky Properties LLC (CSP), a jointly-owned holding company for residential properties that are acquired, resold, or retained in a portfolio. CSP has successfully completed more than 400 renovation or flip properties. I am also a joint owner of Clear Sky Holdings (CSH), which purchases tax lien certificates and offers hard money lending. CSP and CSH also own some commercial properties as well.

My partner, Sam, has extensive experience in a broad variety of real estate endeavors and is especially skilled at working with real estate owned (REO) properties, distressed properties, and financially distressed property owners. Sam has twenty-five years of real estate work experience, having started as a real estate broker part-time during his prior career. He is a licensed real estate broker in Virginia, Maryland, and DC, so he saves us 3 percent or more on every retail sale. He founded Green Dot Realty, a successful independent realty company that we both now own. Sam is also my partner in founding and owning each of the Clear Sky Companies. Sam and I also co-owned a title company earlier in our real estate careers.

Last, but by no means least, Ed Grass retired as a litigation partner from an Am Law 25 firm and now advises the Clear Sky companies. He first had a successful career litigating for and against Fortune 25 companies in federal and state courts around the country, including several federal appeals courts, and state high courts. He also has evaluated, drafted, and litigated hundreds of contracts during his career. Ed started with us knowing little about real estate law, but now analyzes our most complex real estate transactions and has purchased and sold distressed real estate investments along with me and Sam.

Please do not be intimidated by our profiles. We did not start out operating at this level and, most likely, neither will you. That is why we banded together into a team! You can be a salesperson, computer programmer, plumber, personnel supervisor, bank teller, or pretty much anything else when you start on the roadmap. To gain the depth of knowledge essential to becoming successful, the important thing for you to do is to develop a particular focus or market niche. There are no shortcuts or cheat sheets. Wherever you start, you need to invest time in developing a deep understanding of your business area; this is the best way to secure long-term success. You should aim to develop valuable skills and industry expertise that you can apply to any real estate deal. This will also help you attract valuable partners to fill your knowledge gaps. Also, never stop learning. Once you have mastered one particular skill or market area, expand to the next – the wider your knowledge the broader your horizons.

This niche approach is iterative. A single niche is insufficient to expand an investment portfolio indefinitely or react to disruptions. The market frequently changes so, as an investor, you must be able to adjust to new realities. We started with foreclosure fix-and-flips, and built a residential rental portfolio, but always kept expanding outward as we grew our skills and capital. We started hard money lending because we had first taken out such loans ourselves and not only learned how it is done but why and how to improve it.

Distressed assets are at the core of our model, and the many ways to profit from them make up the multiple pathways to our success. These are properties that typically need more fixing than could be reasonably done by a regular homeowner on an average budget and thus are a place you can add value and profit. Or these may be properties that are undervalued or need to be sold quickly without hanging around on the market (if this is the case check for bodies buried in the backyard before you hand over any cash). We actually found human bones in one of our older Washington, DC properties. We called the police and they were not very interested.

If you are new to distressed assets, you'll need to know how to find them, how to secure them, and how to pay for or finance them – and we have multiple chapters devoted to each of these. Just as importantly, you'll want to learn how to spot bad deals and walk away. In fact, our best deals are the ones we walked away from. When all goes well and you successfully purchase a good asset, you'll need to know how to get the best value from your investment, whether that be through rental, retail, wholesale, or lending. There are opportunities to make as well as lose lots of money at every step in a real estate transaction.

Most people have heard of fixing and flipping. However, that is only one method of getting value out of a distressed property, and it might not be the best place to start if you do not have the right circumstances and knowledge base. The truth is unless you have a few thousand in the bank and the necessary skill set or very good contacts to cover a wide range of maintenance and repair jobs, fixing and flipping is probably not yet for you. On the other hand, if you or a partner are a contractor who knows the real-world cost of repairs, but you're not familiar with property law and don't have a real estate license, a fix-and-flip may be the right move for you, potentially as part of a larger team of temporary or long-term partners. You have a big part of the problem solved by knowing your likely repair costs, and the key aspects of securing and selling real property should be pretty easy for you to pick up to make a complete package. If fixing and flipping is not for you, then an alternative might be wholesaling (detailed later in the book).

Finding a Deal

Marketing directly to motivated sellers to find leads is the key both to early- and long-term success. The best bit is that you can start this without a dollar in savings. If you can find a deal, you can sell it without putting in any cash – more on this later. However, you will get nowhere without the deals themselves, and that is why you need to market to motivated sellers. The best investment strategies and bank balances in the world are useless unless you have motivated sellers, which you can source yourself or as part of a team.

The best approach is to cultivate an informal marketplace that is unique to you, which we therefore will cover. This will minimize your competition and allow you to find and win deals that others cannot. Everyone reading this already has a unique position by the very fact that you live somewhere and are part of that community. Every personal relationship or local network you have or can build offers you a place to start. If you can't join a marketplace, simply start your own.

Why do most people fail or quit this business?

We first need to talk about failure precisely because we want you to be successful. Failure is always a possibility, but identifying the elephant in the room and looking it in the eye will allow you to tame it. (A bag of peanuts may come in handy, too). Anyway, there are some key pitfalls to avoid and difficult steps to climb, and we don't want you tripping up. Knowing what to do is only half the story. When working in real estate you also need to know what *not* to do, because mistakes can be very costly and potentially ruinous to your business.

We will always be honest and straight with you, which is why I will tell you that this is not a business for everybody. Nor is it a scheme to get rich fast, with little effort. This is a business for the long haul, and you must be prepared for the slog ahead. We run into about 200 real estate investors a month at various industry events. Roughly 10 percent of them are experienced investors and the rest are new to the business. If you do the math, your next questions should be, "How come 90 percent of these folks are new investors? What happened to the 90 percent of the new investors from previous events who have seemingly disappeared? Why do so many people stop doing this business?" Well, here are the reasons why:

- **You don't know your why**

Most new real estate investors do not fully understand their motivation – their "why?" Why the hell am I putting myself through this? Or their why changes. If you don't know *why* you are in this business, you are unlikely to have the mental fortitude required to endure the steep climb ahead. Before there is success there will be setbacks. Having a good understanding of what drives you toward your goals is essential for building the resilience you'll require.

- **Lack of education**

Some new investors will simply lack the requisite knowledge of the basics. They jump in feet first without doing their homework. However, it is also true that some will be *too* educated, in one field or another, which means they cannot act when they need to because of paralysis by analysis. Ed will tell you that both problems described him early on, which makes sense given his background. Lawyers are trained to be cautious and meticulous and focus on finding problems. Ed still uses those skills but has also learned to pull the trigger on a good real estate deal after a reasonable amount of consideration with the team to assess risk and potential reward. The good news is this book will provide you with the basic information you need to understand residential real estate. So, if you read this to the end, you'll avoid these common pitfalls of knowing too little or being too afraid to act.

- **They don't know how to find deals**

This is a big one. Actually, this may be the hardest step in the process. The bad news is that most real estate books and training programs fail to provide a solution to this common problem, or they'll try to sell you and your competition the same valueless leads that make the 'real estate expert' money but get you nowhere closer to a genuinely good deal. Fortunately for you, this is a key part of our model — *how to find the deals*. In fact, this is the biggest reason we have written this book - to provide real answers that are otherwise lacking in the industry.

- **They don't have the necessary start-up money**

Troubles with start-up cash flow are another big hurdle that many encounter. Often, new investors don't know where to get the money they need to get started. If this is you, fear not, we have some solutions. If you find a good deal there are plenty of ways to make money from the deal without any of your own money or financing in place.

- **Not enough time**

New real estate investors will often fail to dedicate enough time to foundational stages of business development, such as forming a plan or acquiring industry knowledge. Others may simply have poor time management skills. It is rarely a good idea to quit your job and leap headfirst into the world of real estate investment. Sam got his real estate license long before leaving his regular job. If you have enough capital to afford not to work, sure give it a go – but for the most part, you won't so gradual steps are recommended. Our path involves taking the time to learn and work on lead development first, before fully committing to this new journey in life.

- **Failure to assemble a viable team**

Some new investors will fail because they have not built an all-star team. This will often apply to those treading on the more advanced pathway; namely, those wanting to make money from every part of real estate. However, regardless of your pathway, you need to be building your dream team from day one. Ensuring that every knowledge base is covered is one of your best defenses against failure. You may be a contractor but not a real estate broker. You may be a friendly person who likes to meet people and work on leads. You may be a lawyer who knows or can learn real estate law. You may be a real estate agent who can buy and sell property with limited or no commission. You may even check a few of these boxes but to succeed without committing unforced errors, you need *all* of the essential skill sets accounted for with a good team member or at least someone knowledgeable to consult without spending all your money on consultants. So, don't try to be a jack of all trades and master of none – as this is the easiest route to failure.

Don't be intimidated, though, and think you can't do anything until you have everyone. Sam and I started together without an attorney or contractor as a partner. Instead, we tried out people on a given deal to hire or partner on the project. Over time we added Ed as a partner and we have one incredibly skilled contractor we trust completely and use constantly along with a stable of other quality people on a deal-by-deal basis. I'd say you are best off starting at least with one partner, though there are plenty of exceptions such as wholesaling. Even if you and your first partner have similar backgrounds, bouncing ideas off of each other will help you identify and avoid problems, spread risk, and take action on good deals.

- **They give up**

New investors often lack perseverance. Whether you like it or not, you are going to face adversity. Those with a very low-risk tolerance need not apply – we aren't here to bullshit you. Pardon the language, but this is important! Success and great wealth come at a cost and you must be willing to bear it. You are going to have sleepless nights; you are going to be driven close to madness searching for leads that seem never to materialize, but the good news is that this is all part of the plan and all in the learning curve. As long as you modify and correct what you are doing and keep moving forward, you are on the right track and should be proud of yourself for already going well beyond what most people can do.

- **No marketing**

Investors often underspend on marketing or do not spend enough time on free marketing options. The good news is there are lots of free marketing options to get started. We will take you through some of the best options later in this book.

- **No goal setting**

Some new investors fail to create and pursue achievable short-term goals. That's because they are blinded by long-term dreams without the patience or strategy to pursue them logically. Your first goals can be small, something as simple as lead generation. Slow and steady really does win the race, which is why the hare is in a dead-end job while we three tortoises are millionaires many times over. Make your first short-term goal to find leads. If you find five decent leads you are off and running. If that process is not your cup of tea (maybe you are like Ed) you can go to real estate meetups or otherwise look for a possible partner who enjoys that process to work with you even temporarily. Your next short-term goal could be arranging your first wholesale deal. Then maybe set a goal of obtaining and maintaining one rental property that you can leverage to build more. This could be your first goal if you have some savings or a way to raise capital as we discuss later. Wherever you start on our roadmap, if you try to run short-term on long-term goals, you will quickly become dejected and inevitably quit. So, set realistic, incremental targets that fit and work progressively towards larger aspirations.

- **They don't know where to get started**

Lastly, many new investors don't know where to start. Well, the good news here is that you have now already begun as we reach the end of chapter one. Our roadmap will answer the rest for you, so just buckle up and get ready for the ride!

Key Takeaways:

- Figure out your why.
- Get educated in residential real estate investing.
- Learn lead generation (how to find the deals).
- Learn wholesaling and flipping for creating your capital stack.
- Learn hard money lending for creating and closing deals.
- Invest your capital stack to create residual and passive income streams.

Chapter 2

WHAT WILL SET YOU APART: FINDING YOUR KEYS TO WIN AT REAL ESTATE

"Everyone wants to win, but not everyone is willing to prepare to win."
—Bob Knight

"We are what we repeatedly do. Excellence, then, is not an act, but a habit."
—Aristotle

Sometimes, what will set you apart in real estate is your ability to identify good deals and leave the risky and mediocre ones on the table. Taking action in the right direction does make all the difference. One of our colleagues, Raj Prasad, is a great example of this.

Charlie's Story

Raj is an experienced real estate investor, an entrepreneur, and now a good friend of ours. We met Raj, through Charlie, at the courthouse steps bidding on foreclosure auctions. Raj had been a realtor/broker for many years and already had some knowledge in the real estate investing space when we met. He owned his own real estate brokerage with other agents and figured he'd try his hand at buying foreclosed properties. Raj is a lifelong learner. After he keenly observed my strategies for courthouse bidding, we became friends. He knew what asset types I purchased for my team, how much we would pay for them, and eagerly followed the property through the entire process to see how much money we made on the fix and flip outsale, i.e., the sale event when a flipper sells the flipped house to the final buyer. Foreclosures are public events that you too can go and observe anytime and as often as you like just like Raj.

Raj also worked hard to find distressed homes outside of the courthouse auctions, and then fixed and flipped them. He knew by this time Clear Sky had started offering hard money loans. We provided him with 100 percent financing because he got deals with good equity already baked in and spent his own money on the renovations. After fixing and flipping the properties. Raj would make an average profit of $40,000 to $50,000 per house. He would then put that profit back into our pool of hard money mortgages as an investor.

As we gained experience with making hard money loans, we began offering an investment opportunity into our pooled mortgage fund, paying a solid interest return and allowing us to use the money to make hard money loans at higher rates. So, while actively doing fix-and-flips, Raj also became a passive investor generating residual or passive income through our lending business. After putting his profits from one fix-and-flip deal into the hard-money mortgage pool, he would then go find another house and rinse and repeat, using hard money borrowed from us, and make another $50K to invest in our pool. Over time, his passive income grew substantially.

Raj's story illustrates how real estate investing can be a bit like taking money off the gambling table. When you gamble, you're very likely going to lose all your money over time unless you take some money off the table each time you experience a win. In Raj's case, his wins funded his lower-risk investments into our mortgage fund, and his riskier but highly profitable fix-and-flip deals were more like gambling. He used every high result to fund a reliable, residual source of income for the long term. Whatever passive income streams you choose, we believe that method is key to truly successful real estate investing over the long term. Our part in Raj's success story was the birth of our model.

For the last twenty years, I have enjoyed coaching basketball at various levels, including high school, recreational leagues, and the highest AAU levels both as a head coach and assistant coach. Before every game, I'd go over the Keys to the Win with the team. We would watch games or films of our opponent, analyze scouting reports, and consider our strengths and weaknesses. Ed learned and did the same thing as a college football player under top coaches who went on to the pros. This is exactly what *you* need to do when you're mastering your strategy in real estate. Take some time to consider *how* you can be successful and have the guts to look your weaknesses in the eye and work to fix them yourself or by teaming up. Just as importantly, be confident and accept that you are strong in some areas so you use those strengths.

Here is our advice on how to do this:

1. Get Educated

The first key to success is getting educated in real estate basics. We don't necessarily mean formal education. You might not have a high school degree for any number of reasons, but that doesn't mean you can't learn real estate. Conversely, you could have a Ph.D. in physics and not have the patience to learn real estate.

We have already identified a lack of real estate education as a key reason people fail in this business. A sound education is a vital building block for every ambitious investor. Unless you hope to get lucky— and you won't get lucky, by the way—you need to know what you're doing and why before you jump into the market. While there will always be an element of trial and error in any new venture, the basics need to be mastered ahead of time so you have a solid platform from which to defend yourself against the inevitable uncertainties you'll encounter along the way. Simply put: Don't throw money about and hope to learn on the job. Hold fire and curb your enthusiasm for a bit while you get a grip on the necessary know-how—much of which we have helpfully included in this book.

The fundamentals of the education you'll need for successful real estate investing include knowing:

- how to find distressed property
- how to make deals
- how to raise money
- how to grow your team from nothing
- where to specialize
- when to take risk
- how to manage assets (properties, loans, tax lien certificates)
- and much, much more

Honestly, the list goes on and on, and there is no shortcut. If you're serious, get ready to suck it up and start learning a lot.

The good news is that investing in your education now will make everything that follows later much easier. Once you can talk the talk, you can start walking the walk because raising money will no longer seem like a mysterious and impossible task and instead become one achievable step in the process. After you've mastered the essentials and even started on some of the more advanced stuff, there'll always be more to learn! This is an industry that never sleeps, so if you aren't willing to study hard, be prepared for failure.

2. Build a Good Team (virtually or otherwise)

Yes, I already said this and I am going to keep harping on about this. A critical key to success, over time, is to build a team of superstars around you, whether long-term or just for a specific deal. Knowing a little of everything won't get you very far. No man is an island. You need a team of experts if you want to master this game, so divide and conquer, my friends! I have been doing real estate investing well and making a lot of money for a few decades now and I still do not know it all. I still need my team. Your team will need to consist of various types of professionals and subject experts that you are not, including:

- real estate agent(s)
- bankers,
- insurance agent(s)
- bird dog(s)

- private lender(s)
- lawyer(s)
- mentor(s)
- title company(ies)
- contractor(s), and
- someone to take the coffee order (Mine's cream and two sugars, thanks.)

They (whoever they are) say, "Start with what you know." Well, in this case, it's a question of *who* you know. When thinking about team members, first consider your friends, family members, or that guy you went to high school with that you sometimes see popping up on Facebook. I am not telling you to build a family business per se, I am simply asking you to start by looking at the talent pool you have right under your nose. Sam and Ed became friends at their kids' bus stop and now here we are. Your team is out there.

When we first started, Sam and I created a "Green Dot Realty Ring of Fame," which was our version of a football ring of fame. Our goal was to fill in the spaces to form a star-studded lineup. We wanted to do fix-and-flips, so we needed a home improvement guy, a roofer, an electrician, and so on so we could estimate costs associated with possible purchases and then repair profitably. Of course, this took time to evolve – it still is! Patience is a must-have virtue in the world of real estate. Thankfully, we eventually found the right people for each position and had enough of a team to get to work.

But what if you don't have many contacts or those you do have aren't a good fit after all? Don't worry, there are many ways to build a team from scratch, without the luxury of an already bulging address book. For example, I often attend round table RE conventions, which host the best of the best in every category, so the industry participants can network and if they so choose, combine or recruit. These events allow you the opportunity to engage with like-minded people who are looking to share expertise, also known as you scratch my back, I'll scratch yours. Even if you don't make a given connection there you will see examples of the sort of people and the sort of expertise you will want to locate elsewhere.

Of course, you won't necessarily build your dream team after your first draft. Some people won't share your dedication, while others may retire or move on in a different direction. You might pair with an older experienced businessperson and supply the lead generation drive for the team, or vice versa. The three of us happen to be close in age and share a similar outlook which has worked for us. Most importantly, we trust each other's judgment and honesty. Realize that perfection is always a work in progress and just keep the process moving forward. Of course, make every effort to retain anyone who turns out to be a rising star as the fewer replacements you need to make the smoother your evolution will be.

Whichever way it works out for you, we all need to start from somewhere. As Sam often says, "Even if you don't like it, you have to start where you are...there are no other choices." It is better to have a work-in-progress than nothing at all. If none of your original line-up make it to your long-term dream team, that's fine, they played their part and moved on – nothing to dwell over. Maybe you made a bad choice or a given person was a bad fit. Learn from it and refine it as you go.

Finally, do not be afraid to join teams. If you are just starting it might be a better bet to join a team and learn from how they do it— from their best ideas and their mistakes— as you start building your own from the experience. Be honorable though in whatever you do. While it should go without saying, don't steal leads or business opportunities! The idea is to add value to the team while you learn and grow. Your reputation is critical so you want everyone to hear that you are a good, fair, and honest person (because you are), and that will help you develop relationships with other like-minded people who you will want on a team you develop.

You'll be pleased to know we have a whole chapter dedicated to building a team, so more on this later.

3. Assess Your EQ vs. IQ

We are all familiar with the concept of intelligence quotient or IQ – where it is usually assumed, the bigger the better. However, having an Einstein or a Da Vinci on your team won't make you a successful businessperson. Would someone like that be the best for walking around neighborhoods to learn the local real estate situation and chat up people to find leads? Was the smartest kid in your high school ultimately the most successful in business? As a law partner, Ed had many associates from Ivy League schools, but some of the best and most productive came from the top of their class at little George Mason University. Why? Because those students without exception grew up in the real world, worked for everything they got, and knew how to strap up and keep learning and fighting until they reached the finish line and won. Maybe some of the Ivy kids had bigger IQs and could write a more erudite (Ed likes big words!) appellate brief, but that really doesn't matter when you are down in the litigation trenches taking artillery fire!

Often even more important than IQ is EQ; this is the *emotional quotient* we all possess as individuals. While having a high IQ is of course helpful, EQ often is the quality that determines the winners from the losers where business is concerned. EQ is defined as the level of a person's emotional intelligence in four categories: self-awareness, self-management, social awareness, and relationship management.[1] The George Mason law students were all A+ in these categories and were smart, too. Don't feel bad for the Ivy League kids, some of them were OK.

To be successful in real estate investment, you need to be good at all four of these categories – or at least have a partner who fills in where you fall short. Take my family as an example. Out of my parents and four siblings, I am the only one who doesn't possess a master's degree – so on paper, they are outperforming me on IQ. However, their combined net worth equals about 30 percent of mine. I am not trying to disrespect my family. Your balance sheet doesn't determine whether you are a great person or not. I am just demonstrating that IQ isn't always the key to great wealth as my success is largely thanks to my large EQ.

I don't mean to boast, but the fact is that I have been successful. Being able to recognize my strengths and weaknesses has helped me along the way. My time-management skills are optimal. I am emotionally stable and, therefore, resilient. You'll definitely need to know how to take "no" for an answer in this industry, so resilience is essential! I have excellent relationship-building skills within the business world. As a good friend once told me, "You are only as rich as your Rolodex," and that is so true. Hey kids out there, that was a paper spinny thing on which you wrote contact information during the dinosaur era, much like a Contacts app you use on a smartphone. (Sigh.)

Of course, not everyone will have a high EQ, but there are ways around an EQ deficit. I told you teams are important, didn't I? Ed is an invaluable team member because he is a lawyer who is a master at identifying, assessing, and overcoming unusual legal and business issues. However, he would also be the first to tell you he would rather be reading a document while sitting in front of a computer than knocking on doors and networking with strangers. That is part of the reason Ed valued those George Mason students so much. They had some of the EQ that Ed had the guts to admit he was missing.

Ed is not our EQ guy, but that doesn't matter because that's my primary role. This is why the team structure is so vital, we cannot operate optimally without the three of us together. Sam is more like me in that he has a solid EQ. But where I often manage lead generation, Sam uses his form of EQ to pick up the phone and politely but effectively manage contractors, employees, banking relationships, and so on – all the critical business matters under the hood of our business. We also all have enough IQ and EQ to know our limitations and therefore bounce questionable situations and people off each other to reach optimal decisions. When I want to bash someone over the head (metaphorically I swear), I check in with my two guardian angels and they usually tell me to hold on a second.

4. Create Good Habits

Even with a solid team with you behind the ball, you and they will still need some momentum to carry it the full 100 yards needed to score a touchdown. This *momentum* is built through good habits. Every day, within your team, there needs to be active marketing, relationship building, industry research, deal analysis, deal execution, and so on. The three of us enjoy having lunch with each other now and again as an easy way to keep up to date and collaborate on the big picture and any problematic details of what each person is doing in between Zoom calls, emails, and texts. It sounds simple, but it is critical.

Like the movie *Groundhog Day*, you're going to have to get familiar with certain key tasks day in and day out. For example, you cannot afford to let your foot off the gas with marketing just because you have managed to accelerate a deal over the line and you are busy executing it. The pipeline to future deals needs to be continually maintained and developed, even if you have a load of deals currently in hand. The industry can be volatile at times, so it's best to fix the roof when the sun is shining.

For example, it took us several years to understand and make a profit with tax liens, but that investment of time was well-spent because it generated returns when we needed them most. Had we waited for one of the many real estate downturns to start learning, we would not have been able to generate profits there to keep the lights on. When tax lien investing became an optimum use of our funds due to overall market conditions we had learned and done enough that we were more than ready to move in a big pile of chips.

Same thing with our hard money business. We slowly developed the knowledge, contract language, experience, outside counsel, etc., to execute some small deals. As we learned and dealt with some problem loans, we became more confident and were ready to shift a lot of money there as the number of available foreclosures fell and the profit margins became thin. By loaning money to fix-and-flippers, we essentially created a virtual lead generation of dozens looking for deals that we could make money on by financing rather than buying, fixing, and selling ourselves.

This business has a relatively fast turnaround to profit on each loan compared to the gains from tax lien investing which can take two to three years in some cases.

Your routine should always be focused on moving things forward and anticipating the next opportunity. Of course, if you are trying the same techniques over and over and not making headway, then change it up. But remember, ultimately consistent execution of what is working and planning for the next wave is the key to ongoing success. You need to create both short-term and long-term goals and then methodically construct your daily schedule to meet these ends.

Self-Assessment

Okay, we are making good progress, but before you go any further, I would like you to conduct a little self-assessment. I started doing this early on and I continually reassess where I am to decide what I need to learn next and where I want to go. You too need to figure out where you sit today regarding your knowledge as a real estate investor. Below, we have provided five different familiarity levels along with descriptions. It's your job to place yourself at one of these levels. Doing so will help you navigate your way through the rest of this book without being held up by details you have already grasped or getting bewildered by jargon you aren't quite ready to decipher. Let's go!

Level One: Kindergarten Investor

You're a kid in a toy store, with your eyes on that shiny new model race car, begging your parents to buy it for you. At this early stage, you'll still be looking through rose-tinted glasses at the prospect of buying and selling houses, like it's a real-life Monopoly game, and you are eager to play your first roond. This is the very beginning stage of real estate investing. Perhaps your plan is just to buy a property and let the money roll in and that's the extent of your plan so far. Well, if this is you, keep reading every word, there is a long, bumpy but exciting road ahead.

Level Two: Elementary Investor

You're a student in your early years of school, and you're just starting to learn the basics of real estate investing. You still have a lot of questions and will probably need a fair bit of guidance along the way. You understand that owning property requires more than just a one-time payment and that there are expenses and responsibilities that come with being a landlord or property owner. Perhaps you are feeling a bit overwhelmed at this stage. But don't worry, that's normal. You know enough to realize this is a serious life decision and need much more detail before you can tell if this is a real possibility for you. Well, what do you know? A lot of that detail is in this book.

Level Three: Intermediate Investor

You're starting to find your footing in the real (estate) world. You're getting more comfortable with evaluating properties and running the numbers, you're starting to see some success in your investments, and you're comfortable negotiating deals. You have a good understanding of the local real estate market and know how to find good investment opportunities. At this stage, you're feeling more confident that this business can be successful. Our model will help you realize and optimize that success.

Level Four: High-level Investor

This is the stage where real estate investing becomes a serious business. You're a seasoned pro who's been around the block a few times. You know the ins and outs of real estate investing and have a track record of success to back it up. You are skilled at finding and closing complex deals and likely have a team of professionals working for you, including real estate agents, lawyers, accountants, and contractors. You now want to learn new ways to find deals and make money in your field. Well, what do you know? We have some insights for you as well that we are confident will be new to you.

Level Five: Pro-level Investor

You're a superstar athlete at the top of your game, and you're reading this book for pleasure alone. You've achieved a level of success that most people can only dream of and you're pushing yourself to be even better. You are adept at navigating the market, finding the best deals, and negotiating the most favorable terms. You may well have a vast portfolio of properties that generate passive income, allowing you to focus on growing your business and pursuing new investments.

If you are a pro then you may just be reading this to beat your competition and find a few new tips and tricks. Good on you: That's the fighting spirit! We think as a pro you'll definitely up your game by reading our book and potentially learn entirely new areas to profit from such as tax liens or pooled mortgage investing. For everyone else, we know the remainder of this book will teach you much that is entirely new, give you a new perspective, or perhaps tell you everything you need to know before diving into real estate investing.

Key Takeaways:

- Invest in your education
- Build a strong team
- Assess your EQ vs. IQ
- Create good habits
- Do a self-assessment to determine your investor level
- Cultivate your spirit of perseverance

---

1. https://www.simplypsychology.org/emotional-intelligence.html.

Chapter 3
GOAL SETTING

"Greatness is not measured by what a man or woman accomplishes, but by the opposition he or she has overcome to reach his or her GOALS."
— Dorothy Height

Sam's Story

When I started flipping properties with Charlie, we needed to get access to capital. This was in 2003, when the hard money investor community was very small and in a nascent state, at least in our area. Our goal was to get a bank line of credit. It was a challenge, to say the very least. First, we spent quite a while putting our personal financial information together in a way that could be readily understood by bankers. Next, we started talking to bankers and loan officers. I remember one day we got ourselves dressed up and went to talk to a banker in his impressive office building. In hindsight, I guess it was impressive that we even scored a meeting. However, he said no so fast that we didn't even have time to show him our financials. What we were learning was that not all banks had an appetite for doing fix-and-flip loans. Further, even if they liked our pitch, we learned that not all bankers could advocate for us effectively at their loan committee meeting and secure a deal for us. But we could only learn this through trial and error.

We then learned fairly quickly that community banks were the only institutions that had an appetite for the kind of loan we wanted. A loan officer needs to be very well connected at a community bank before the loan committee will take a new client seriously. We had to have a seamless financial package that was easily understandable to quickly hand off to a banker so that we could explain our financial position and plans for the future. Nevertheless, we got our financials and plans together and then started to research. I started with the Yellow Pages. Are you old enough to remember that big yellow phone book? I looked under "banks" and began with the As. Cross-referencing information on the internet, I checked to see if the bank met the capital requirements to qualify as a community bank. Next, I began researching loan officers listed at the banks that I could meet.

Lucky for me, my first real hit came up when I got to the Bs. I found Burke and Herbert who coincidentally were located near me. I noticed that one of the board members of the bank had the same last name as one of the junior loan officers. That loan officer was a young man named Joe Collum. I figured that Joe might have a bit more influence than the average loan officer. I was right! I called him and he told me that they had an interest. Yes! I then took the financial package I had in hand and overnighted it to him. Within a week we had an initial approval for our first commercial loan. As I write this paragraph some twenty years later, Charlie and I have lunch scheduled with that same Joe!

The lessons here: You need a goal. You then need specific objectives under the goal. Finally, you need to break that goal down into manageable tasks. Most importantly, never forget that lasting relationships are a lot of fun and help you build a great portfolio.

Now, you cannot throw a bunch of darts into space and expect to hit the bullseye. Hard work needs to be focused, and that's why we need to talk about goal setting. Think of it as playing a guitar without tuning the strings. You can strum away to your heart's content and produce sound, but it's going to be discordant. Tuning your instrument is akin to setting your goals— the finished product will be melodic, polished, and perfected–so all the hard work won't be in vain. That's two analogies and we're only on the first paragraph! I'm spoiling you, I really am.

Goals are also useful for setting momentum. Without something to aspire to, you'll be working hard for the sake of working hard. That sounds about as inspiring as cold porridge. A strong vision of where you need to be makes a rough plan an actionable plan and prevents you from becoming derailed by endless distractions. Without an achievable goal in place, we can become so focused on perfecting every fringe detail that we never get close to completing anything at all.

Within the world of real estate investment, goal setting can help you make smart decisions about which properties to invest in, or avoid, and how to manage them effectively. For example, if your goal is to generate passive income from rental properties, you'll want to focus on finding properties that are likely to attract reliable, long-term tenants. On the other hand, if your goal is to flip properties for a profit, you'll need to be more focused on finding properties with the potential for significant appreciation in value that a homebuyer would want for their family.

I first set my goals about sixteen years ago. But just as we evolve as people over time, our goals need to evolve, too. Therefore, I make a point of revisiting my goals from time to time to adjust them to my present-day reality. Real ambition is drawn from goals that are never really completed because they are always growing into something bigger and better. I like to use a question-and-answer format to set and develop my goals. However, you're welcome to use whichever system works best for you. Below is my ten-year plan, which I created in 2004:

Work-Related Goals

Q: What income level do I desire?

A: I will have an income level over $300k annually per year in 2004 dollars.

Q: What responsibility do I seek?

A: I will be in control of assets valued between $5 million and $10 million.

Q: What authority will I command?

A: I will have the respect of those who work with me and for me because I treat them in a humanistic way.

Q: What prestige will I gain from work?

A: My business successes and honest dealings will establish me as a contributing member of my community.

Home Goals

Q: What standard of living will I provide for my family and myself?

A: There shall be no member of my family, nuclear or extended, whom I cannot enable with my resources.

Q: What kind of house will I live in?

A: My home will be a place that I share with my family where we can go and reflect, and it will be a place where others can come to forget their troubles and grow with me.

Q: What kind of vacations will I take?

A: My vacations will broaden my thinking and surround me with new experiences that are joyful to me and to my family and friends.

Q: What financial support will I provide for my children?

A: I will enable my children to actively pursue their professional dreams, unconditionally.

Social Goals

Q: What kinds of friends do I want to have?

A: I will have friends from every walk of life. They will be from a broad range of social, economic, and occupational areas.

Q: What social groups do I want to join?

A: I will assist in community redevelopment projects.

Q: What community leadership positions would I like to hold?

A: I will be on the board of directors or the chair of an organization that is focused on a community revitalization project.

Q: What worthwhile causes do I want to champion?

A: I will contribute my time and resources to local service organizations that improve education and access to medicine for people who cannot access them on their own.

You should notice all of my goals listed above are supported by specific objectives. Having goals doesn't mean you need to follow the formality of a project plan. However, you do need to consider the big goals and big objectives. Sometimes a single objective can feel like an ever-changing labyrinth of tasks. Once completed, some tasks will lead to new tasks that weren't anticipated before. All this complexity needs to be organized within goals and objectives so you can review your progress easily and make sure you are going in the right direction. If the tasks you are completing aren't serving your goals and objectives, you need to revise your goals and objectives accordingly or review your list of tasks.

I'm sure you're thinking, "But how long does this all take us, Sam?" Well, it takes a lifetime. This methodology offers you a framework through which you can structure your life and in doing so, produce results that are consistent with your values and goals.

Remember the Stoics? They'll be before your time as much as mine. Nevertheless, the philosophy of Stoicism, developed by our hard-nosed antecedents, has enjoyed somewhat of a renaissance of late. Stoicism was founded around 300 B.C., and those who practice it believe that virtuous behavior is enough to achieve a well-lived, fulfilled life because they believe that "virtue is the only good." Essentially, virtuous living is good for humans, and everything else–from health to hedonism–is neither good nor bad in and of itself but is only as good or as bad as you make them by your responses to them. If you respond to something negative in a virtuous way, for example, then you have made that negative thing positive for your life. As you can imagine, for the Stoics, goal setting was essential for living a meaningful life; this was achieved through self-discipline, self-control, and endurance.

I took this philosophy and applied it to my own life, with a few adjustments to suit a twenty-first-century man. Not everything the ancient philosophers did necessarily translates to today, after all! Epictetus recommended saying, "Tomorrow you will die," to your kids as you tucked them in bed. While I believe instilling resilience in children is good, that kind of fatalism is a little excessive in modern America. Plus, one of your goals would then have to be saving for the inevitable therapy sessions. However, there are a lot of sound ideas we can learn from the Stoics, who believed setting and pursuing goals is not about achieving external success or accolades, but rather about cultivating inner peace and living by following one's values.

Epictetus wrote extensively about goal setting in his *Enchiridion*. He believed that, while setting goals was important, we should be careful about how we approach the process. He cautioned against becoming too attached to our goals, reminding us that our ultimate goal should be to live following our values, not just to achieve external success. He said, "Don't set your heart on so many things...if you do, you are bound to be a slave to them."[1] In other words, if we become too focused on achieving a specific outcome, we may lose sight of what really matters. This means setting goals that are based on our efforts and actions, rather than external factors that we cannot control.

> *"The first and most important field of philosophy is the application of principles such as 'not to lie.'...the second field is that of the training grounds themselves — the gymnasium and the playing field."*
> *—Epictetus, Greek Stoic philosopher*

By cultivating our character, rather than worrying about external outcomes, we can achieve great success without compromising our values and becoming despondent in our pursuit of greatness.

Another key aspect of Stoic goal setting is the importance of accepting failure and setbacks. We all screw up, it's part of being human. Unfortunately, so is self-damnation which is a surefire way of losing our focus. The Stoics believed that failure was an inevitable part of life and that we should learn to accept it with grace and use it as an opportunity to learn and grow. See, they had a softer side when they weren't giving their children nightmares! Seneca, another Roman philosopher, wrote, "A gem cannot be polished without friction, nor a man perfected without trials." So, in essence, we shouldn't be discouraged by obstacles or setbacks but, instead, use these experiences as opportunities to improve ourselves. It's like growing muscle; you have to tear it a little before you get stronger.

The Stoics also believed in the importance of living in the present moment and focusing on the process of achieving our goals rather than becoming fixated on the end result. How many times have you failed to realize a dream because you never got going with the first of the tasks in front of you? Epictetus wrote, "Don't set your mind on things you can't control but focus on what you do control and make it better." In other words, we should focus on the things that are within our power to control and work to improve them rather than becoming fixated on outcomes that may be outside of our control. If it's your dream to become a real estate tycoon, cool, but you need the motivation to plow through thousands of tasks to meet multiple milestones before you'll get anywhere close to this end goal. Wanting and believing is all well and good, but those actions must be accompanied by sound strategy and a hell of a lot of resilience.

Goal setting is one of the most important things you will do to ensure your success. Indeed, one element that all successful people have in common is their ability to set specific goals and have a plan for achieving them. This means that they can determine exactly what they want and know how they are going to get there. While a kid dreams of going to Disneyland, their dreams are only realized by the planning of their parents, who buy the tickets, book the flights, arrange the accommodation, etc. Big ideas are dependent on little details, there is no shortcut to success. If you want to be a successful real estate investor forget about shortcuts, and embrace the daily grind with the knowledge that it's getting you closer to your dream.

There are three basic types of goal setting:

1. Improvement goals

Improvement goals are focused on personal growth and development. This type of goal-setting is often centered around improving a skill or behavior and is intended to help individuals become better at something over time. For example, an improvement goal might be to read one new book every month to expand one's knowledge on a particular topic or to practice a new skill every day to improve proficiency.

The benefit of improvement goals is that they can lead to a sense of mastery and accomplishment as an individual makes progress toward becoming better at something. They also encourage a growth mindset, which emphasizes the idea that skills and abilities can be developed over time with effort and practice. For example, an improvement goal for a real estate investor might be to improve their ability to identify under-valued properties or negotiate deals with sellers. Other improvement goals might include developing a deeper understanding of real estate market trends or learning about new financing options that could help fund real estate investments.

2. Achievement goals

This type of goal-setting is focused on a specific outcome or result. These types of goals are usually focused on external rewards such as winning a swimming competition or receiving a promotion. For example, an achievement goal might be to earn a specific degree or certification or to launch a successful business.

The benefit of achievement goals is that they can provide motivation and direction as individuals work toward a specific outcome. However, there can also be drawbacks to achievement goals, particularly if an individual becomes too focused on the outcome and loses sight of the importance of the process of achieving it. It's important to balance achievement goals with improvement goals to cultivate a growth mindset and enjoy the journey of personal and professional development.

Achievement goals are also highly relevant to real estate investing as they offer specific outcomes that real estate investors should be aiming to achieve. These might include acquiring a certain number of properties within a given timeframe, achieving a certain level of cash flow or rental income, or increasing the value of a property through renovation or other improvements. Achievement goals can provide motivation and direction for real estate investors but it's important to balance these goals with an appreciation for the process of investing and the importance of long-term financial stability.

3. Financial goals

Financial goals focus on the financial reward that comes with completing or achieving a goal. If you are already super rich and have ventured into real estate out of boredom, I suggest you get a less stressful hobby, perhaps golf or flower arranging, whatever floats your boat. For the rest of us, money is always going to be at the heart of our goals, as glory alone won't pay your kids' college tuition. Financial goals can include saving a certain amount of money, paying off debt, or achieving a specific level of income or net worth.

My financial goals are a great example of this. This type of goal setting should provide you with a sense of financial security and stability and can help individuals achieve their long-term financial objectives with less anxiety hanging over them. However, you need to remember that it's important to approach financial goal setting in a balanced way to avoid becoming too fixated on financial outcomes at the expense of other aspects of life. If you hyperfocus on financial success and goal setting, you are probably going to be disengaging with other more important aspects of your life. Family time, leisure, and personal interests are important ingredients in a balanced life. If you neglect these areas to focus on money alone, you'll find yourself richer but wonder why you ever wanted this wealth in the first place.

Balanced and proportionate financial goals are a critical component of real estate investing. Real estate investing for many represents the pursuit of passive income and building wealth over the long term. Financial goals for real estate investors might include achieving a certain level of monthly cash flow from rental properties, paying off debt associated with real estate investments, or building a portfolio of properties with a certain overall value. While financial goals can be motivating, it's important to remember that real estate investing also involves risk. Financial success should be balanced with an appreciation for the potential challenges and uncertainties of the real estate market.

But don't let these warnings put you off! Instead, see them as sound advice that will better your chances for success. We are only writing this book because we acted on the advice we offer and made a ton of money as a result. It will be hard work and there are risks but the reward is very real for those willing to play by the rules.

Overall, when setting effective goals, there are a few steps you need to follow. First, you need to be specific about the goals that you want to set. You should have a thoroughly written out plan of every detail relating to your goal(s). This allows you to visualize the goal itself so you can act in a fashion that will best facilitate your overall agenda. Next, you need to set a completion date. Doing so will allow you to work with a timeline to prevent procrastination and maintain momentum. I think I did this pretty well. I gave myself a ten-year timeline with a yearly check-in when I set my goals. My success has been thanks to my consistency in following this. This consistency stopped me from becoming complacent or going off track. The truth is my goals continue to shift and change as I grow within the industry, and check-ins allow me to adapt my goals appropriately. Ed has told me he would do a complete reassessment every two years on whether he wanted to continue practicing law in a huge law firm and his alternative options. Did he really want to work all those hours with the sacrifices that entailed? What about going to be corporate counsel in-house for less money but fewer hours and more free weekends? How about becoming a monk? No really, one of Ed's partners actually did that.

Once you have set a completion date, you need to devise a plan for reaching the overarching goal. In my case, this is my ten-year plan. I use this plan to track my progress and make sure I don't miss out on any crucial tasks along the way to achieving the end result. Finally, you need to figure out where and with whom you will be accomplishing these goals.

Let's look at how we have a goal and break it into its short and long-term components. The first goal on my list was that I'd like to have an income equal to $300,000 in 2004 dollars. At first, this seems pretty specific, but once I dug down into it I realized it wasn't nearly specific enough to set underlying objectives. First, what income? Is it what I list as adjusted gross income on my tax return? Does that consider long-term savings? Does that consider the gains and losses that are just on paper in my real estate portfolio? In hindsight, it was a goal that could have had a lot of supporting details. Had I written down the details, it might have looked something like this:

I will have:

- Adjusted gross income (AGI) in 2004 dollars to be equal to $300,000.
- Growth of my retirement savings by no less than $50,000 annually.
- Generate 50 percent of my AGI income from passive or close to passive business investment income.

Now that my goal is broken down more specifically, I can work on shorter-term goals. For example: My 2004 AGI is $186,872. I need to get focused on bringing this number up incrementally over ten years. Without accounting for any inflation adjustments, in 2004 I needed to start increasing my income by $11,313 annually to meet my goal in ten years. This was only a 6 percent increase, which seems quite achievable. That means I only needed to expend the same work effort as I did in 2004 and be 6 percent more economically efficient at it to meet my 2005 goal. This is a short-term goal. It is achievable and perhaps, seeing it in hindsight, I realize that it is not nearly aggressive enough.

Anyhow, knowing what I know now, below the 6 percent increase goal I can break it down to something like this: "In order to achieve this goal, we need to flip one additional house in 2005 and reduce our holding time of flip assets by 15 percent. To do one more flip, we need to do three more mailing campaigns. To reduce our holding time of assets, we need to consolidate contractors and pay a single general contractor to manage the workflow more efficiently. Then, we will be able to achieve our 6 percent increase goal." I expect by now you are starting to see how we can start with a long-term goal and break it down into achievable objectives that will support our success.

We Follow Seven Keys to Goal Achievement:

Desire, Belief, Knowledge, Opportunity, Vision, Planning, and Commitment

Now, here are six action steps for when new real estate investors feel lost:

1. Do a self-assessment
2. Stay focused
3. Find a mentor
4. Partner up
5. Set short-term goals
6. Consume good material (in real life or online)

Key Takeaways:

- Set your goals.
- Set smaller objectives within each goal.
- Determine your timeline for achieving a measured goal.
- Take action towards your objectives.
- If you achieve forward progress, repeat. If you don't, adjust your approach.
- Periodically reassess if your desires and goals have changed.

---

1. Epictetus, *The Enchiridion,* independently published, June 2017.

Chapter 4
BUILD YOUR TEAM

"From the first person I hired, I was never the smartest guy in the room. . . . And if you're going to be a leader . . . and you're the smartest guy . . . in the room, you've got real problems."
—Jack Welsh

If you don't agree with the above statement or even see its value, then I think you will have a very hard time being successful in the business of real estate investing. As with every business, a successful real estate business is a team sport. The best teams win the most, and the best leaders surround themselves with smarter people than themselves all the time. It is that simple.

Side note: When I say "smart," I don't only mean "book smart." I mean "book smart" and "street smart." Basically, an alternative way to say IQ and EQ, though there is a lot of overlap between the two. Overall, you need to have a team built of people with practical sense and diligence. If you have a genius IQ, that is helpful. However, it is not a necessary component for moving through the real estate pathways. There is no aspect of real estate ownership and management that can't be mastered over time. Anyone working in the field needs to apply themselves and take time to understand their role in the process. When you see someone who is thriving in their role, you are seeing years of practice and refinement at work.

I can tell you that we are always working on building the best team possible. It is an evolving process. We have come a long way in our twenty years, but there is always room for improvement. It can seem daunting when someone is just starting out. But forming a great team is incredibly important at any stage of the game, especially early on. Remember, your team will evolve as *you* evolve. Still, you want to do your best to start off on the right foot with the right people. Before you go out and form a team, I highly encourage you to determine your niche, your market, and your strategy. I don't care if you get the smartest people in a room and begin working with them. If you are not focused and super clear on *your* plan and strategy, then no team member will be able to help you. The more specific you are, the better people will be able to help you achieve your goals. So, here is a roadmap from A to Z of key people you need on your team for optimal success:

1. Mentor

Your mentor might be a real estate professional or another investor. They should be someone you can relate to that is vested in your success. A person with related real estate experience and a strong network will accelerate your success.

2. CPA

A certified public accountant is qualified to give advice related to tax accounting. Your local CPA who prepares your taxes is a great source of information. They can share with you the benefits of using depreciation, long-term gain deferrals, and expense write-offs to raise your real income and reduce your tax liability. Once you get more sophisticated, you might need a CPA to help execute more complicated tax minimization strategies like cost segregation.

3. Attorney(s)

You can't find the best attorney in the world because Ed is already on our team. (I wish Ed would stop editing my section of the book). Ed effectively helps as our general counsel and directs the legal actions taken by outside counsel. Ed is focused on our business. He answers the phone when Charlie and I call. He then immediately takes action. This is very hard to find with outside counsel and very expensive if you do.

You need to get started more modestly by identifying a reliable closing attorney who can give you detailed information about title work and transfers. An attorney who is invested in your success is critical to closing deals. Once you have some properties, you will need a real estate attorney to help you with leasing and evictions. There are many other attorneys that you might employ along the way. To get started, find a good closing attorney. They could become your Ed, or just be paid to do a great job on title and closings.

4. Banker

You will need a traditional banker to handle your money who can send wires, take your phone calls, and maybe get you a home equity line of credit (HELOC) on your house. Find someone local who wants to see your financial stability grow. We recommend starting with a community bank that has a portfolio of local real estate.

5. Insurance Agent

You want an insurance agent who is readily available and is looking out for your needs. They have to ask you the right questions, such as, "Is this property going to be vacant?" Getting the right agent enables you to get the right policy so you have coverage when you need it.

6. Hard Money Lender

Some new investors will rely heavily on a hard money lender when they get started. Other newbies will be reluctant to use hard money. Regardless, you want to have options when you are financing your deals. With some deals, having a hard money lender makes sense; with other deals, it does not make sense. Again, it is helpful to find a hard money lender that you are comfortable with, who you trust, and who trusts you—again, *before* you find your deal.

7. Private Money Lender or Equity Partner

This can be a family friend or someone you know who has enough free cash flow that they can invest their cash alongside your sweat equity and capital investment. If you have a good partner, you can buy more and do more than if you try to "go it alone."

8. Real Estate Agent(s)

Find the highest-performing real estate agents in your local market and talk to them about selling your investment properties. They might be a good source for deals, and if they bring you a deal you can always give them the listing. That way they might get a listing, a sale, and another listing. We call this a triple header. What agent would turn that down?

9. Wholesaler(s)

There is an entire group of people who don't want to fix and flip assets and they are not licensed real estate agents. They look for deals and pass them along to other investors for a fee. That is a wholesaler. Get to know a lot of wholesalers and look through their deals to see if one of them will work for you.

10. Bird Dog(s)

In our real estate community, a bird dog is someone who brings us a deal because they don't want to handle it themselves. Our bird dogs have been wholesalers, agents just getting into the business, neighbors of distressed assets, and pretty much anyone who knows that we buy and sell houses. Let everyone, possible bird dogs, know how they can help you find deals and how they can be rewarded.

11. Title Company

You will need a company that will take your phone call and close a deal fast. They need to be thorough and responsive. This seems like a reasonable standard to achieve. However, in our market, they are few and far between. Identify a good title company before you need to call on them. We have a wonderful title attorney, Rick Oppenheim Jr., whom Sam has known for a while. He was very instrumental in our early and long-term success because he could close on a pre-foreclosure purchase in three days or less. He was also very good with estate sales and anything with a complicated title. I have been told by more than one person that Rick does not get motivated unless Clear Sky calls.

12. Well-Connected Business Professional(s)

If you are in the business long enough you will need business services of every variety. When you meet lawyers, take their names and make notes. When you meet the owner of a tree trimming business, write their name down. Once you have a good list of contacts, you might not have the name of the exact person you will need; but you will have a list of people who will know where to find that person. Make sure they know what you do: buy distressed property.

13. General Contractor

A general contractor is a licensed professional who knows the building code and can contract with other contractors who are licensed for specific trades such as electrical, plumbing, and mechanical work. A good general contractor will be able to guide you as to the scope and cost of getting home improvement work complete, and therefore what repair expenses to expect for a potential distressed property purchase.

14. Plumber

Fortunately, many rehabs only require minor plumbing repairs and improvement. However, if you need to connect to public water, add a bathroom, or replace all of your pipes, you will need to know a good plumber who is reliable and has fair pricing. The big-name companies tend to be neither.

15. General Handyman

This person is going to be able to change bath and electrical fixtures, add trim to a room, paint your house, and do small general repairs. They are well suited to solving smaller problems and doing smaller renovations.

16. Electrician

Any house more than thirty years old is going to probably need an upgraded electrical service. If you are doing major electrical work or electrical work that requires a permit, you will need to find a good electrician, again one who is reliable and has fair pricing. How will you know that? Get to know some electricians.

17. Pest Control Company

You can fix some pest problems yourself, but if you have a bad infestation of roaches, termites, or bed bugs, you will need to know what pest control company is best to call.

18. Cleaning Company

All cleaning is not the same. Getting a house cleaned after construction work is a lot more intensive than having your home swept up. A professional cleaner will have blowers, vacuums, and equipment that you would not use every day. Look for the best cleaning company you can find, one that knows how to clean a house and its windows inside and out, and deal with any unusual debris. It is not uncommon to get a distressed property filled to the gills with every manner of broken furniture and more. Here you can hire some inexpensive moving companies like Two Guys and a Truck or some strong guys in your neighborhood and rent them a truck. Either way, make sure the crew you get is prepared for and wants to deal with an unusual mess, what is commonly called a "trash out."

19. Property Manager

There is a point at which you will need a professional property manager. If you have more than four properties, you will probably be cost-justified in employing a company to manage your properties. If you have more than thirty properties, you can hire your own property manager to work directly for you. Someone has to help out the tenants with repairs, move-in, move-out, and utility issues, which can be very time-intensive. A professional property manager can relieve a lot of stress, provide a good rental experience for your tenants, and leave you to find and fix distressed assets for a bigger return on the use of your time and growing expertise.

20. Accountability Group

You should share your goals and challenges with a core group of people who will provide you with honest feedback on your mistakes and accomplishments. This group of people will hold you accountable to your objectives and goals without being personally judgmental. Sometimes you can spend time either making excuses for your performance shortfalls or hyper-focusing on problems. A group of people who hold you accountable to your goals will help you see beyond those excuses and problems and help you identify fixes.

Overall, if you want to be successful in this business you need to build a great team around you as you might have noticed before in our book. Even if you like to think of yourself as a jack of all trades, you won't be able to build a truly successful portfolio working alone. Take it from me: Without the talents of Charlie and Ed, I wouldn't be nearly as rich as I am, and I have been pretty helpful to them as well. We are a team and we are far greater together than the sum of our parts. If you look at us as a family, we three are like brothers, but we depend on our extended family, too. And just like our team, your team should include real estate agents, bankers, insurance agents, bird dogs, private lenders, lawyers, mentors, contractors, and potentially more. Some will be involved almost daily, while others will appear now and then like distant cousins for special events. If you grow big enough, some of these roles will need to be duplicated, but first, concentrate on finding your starting lineup and work from there.

Right now, I can hear you saying, "Okay Sam, I get it, I need a team. But where the hell do I start?" I realize this can seem like a daunting task because this is not like asking your friends to play a round of golf. But fear not dear reader, anyone can build a team if they follow our advice and keep at it. As I mentioned earlier, professional meetups or professional speed dating types of events are key if you want to find people with similar interests to you. The more networking the better, as you are looking for nine or ten people to join forces with you in some fashion—some with professional experiences outside your current knowledge or beyond your comprehension. So, just like a lot of this business, it's a learning exercise. However, don't overlook what you might already have at hand. Building a relationship is hard work, so utilizing any contacts you already have can save you a lot of time and effort. Ask yourself, "Who do I already have in my network that can offer the experience, skills, expertise, or personality I need in my business?"

If the answer is not your immediate friends and family, what about friends of friends? Referrals are a legitimate way to mine your social network for talent. When you start seeking referrals, you need to be clear about what you are looking for. Be specific about the role you are trying to fill and the qualifications you require for it.

After establishing the kind of roles you need to fill on your team, the next step is to complete due diligence on eligible candidates you find through referrals or personal networking. Sometimes this is as simple as reviewing the person's resume and portfolio or conducting a phone or in-person interview of them or their references. Additionally, you may also want to consider running a background check to ensure that the person is trustworthy and reliable. A team is only as strong as the weakest link, so a bad hire could jeopardize your whole dynamic.

When asking your contacts for reputable referrals, it can also be helpful to ask them if they know anyone to avoid. This level of vigilance early on can save you time and trouble down the road. Think about red flags that suggest an individual wouldn't fit well in your team; these early days of business development will require an all-hands-on-deck mentality. You need people who are conscientious, committed, and willing to learn. If you make a mistake and hire someone who doesn't fit your team... really, don't waste time—tell them! Let them go and find another teammate.

When you are building your list of potential team members, resist the temptation to value people only by what they can offer you. Although this may sound counterintuitive, you need to ask yourself what *you* can offer *them*. When you focus on giving, rather than just receiving, your relationships with your team members will bear much more fruit.

As with any business, you need to be aware of sharks in the water when you're out fishing for contacts. You know that insurance guy who tries to sell policies that sound too good to be true or a plumber who quotes 30 percent below market rates? Well, they typically are a bad choice. Don't get carried away by the excitement of all the new opportunities; you need to be prudent and discerning from day one. Do your homework (it was a myth that this ends the day you graduate high school), seek out recommendations, and consult with references. A resume only tells half of the story; you need to speak to people who have experienced your candidates in a working relationship. It is not good to hire someone because they aced all their college exams if they lack interpersonal skills, turn up late, or have a history of job-hopping.

The way we've built our business is by giving and then giving some more long before we ever expect to receive. This isn't charity or bad business because the harvest that comes as a result of this practice will be far greater the more seeds we have sown (seemed the right time for an agricultural metaphor). Trust us: This works. For example, by giving away free information or education, we create meaningful engagements with individuals and organizations who can then help us down the line. I'm not trying to go all new-age on you; this is how networking has always worked. You've heard it a million times: "We'll scratch your back..." and you know the rest. As a newbie in the world of real estate you may feel you have very little to offer, so don't over-analyze this process. Just give what you do have at your disposal, even if it's something as simple as a listening ear. The more you learn along the way, the easier it will be to find places where you can offer value. All of this will go a long way towards building lasting relationships which is what you need from your future team.

Once you have established a small team, you can look forward to smooth sailing. Just kidding! There's no time to rest on your laurels. Soon you'll want to think about expanding—you're reading this book because you're ambitious, right? Expansion can be facilitated through a multitude of avenues, including some you won't have considered.

Of course, not everyone can form their own teams; some of us need to be joiners. This is what Ed, The Lawyer, did when he joined our team in 2008. He started by providing us with prompt and effective legal analysis and plainly worded answers until eventually we realized we couldn't live without him. Okay, we could live without him but thank God we haven't had to. Have you ever heard of the *two* amigos? More to the point, trying to hire an outside lawyer who immediately picks up the phone every time you call and gives you an actual answer without being mealy-mouthed or saying your chances are fifty-fifty, and charging a fortune, is not easy. We quickly realized that the three of us worked well together as the core of a functioning team focused on the same goals with each bringing something to the table that the other two didn't have. This was a much bigger shift for us than you might otherwise think. If you are going to have more than two partners, particularly when two have already been successful, you have to be absolutely sure that all of your goals align closely. That way there aren't misunderstandings. We have been very fortunate to have a close alignment of goals and all of us work to clarify our goals and objectives so we are all working in the same direction.

In our early team-building stage, when Charlie and I were both working as real estate agents, he would ask me for referrals. At this point, I was working under Green Dot Realty. He'd call me, as a source he trusted, to see if I had recommendations on everyone from landscapers to electricians. Similarly, he'd be one of the first I would call if I wanted some reliable support in closing a deal. Eventually, we realized we would be much stronger if we combined forces. From that moment onwards, we plotted to take over the world (of real estate investment). We are a few hundred trillion short of that dream, but our piece is great and that still leaves a whole lot for you.

This leads me to the story of how we found our favorite electrician and contractor, Maurice. A master electrician by trade, Maurice was working as a landscaper at a friend's company. I spotted him in my neighborhood one day, 200 feet up an industrial telephone pole, fixing wiring and installing a new light. Anyone with the knowledge and guts to do that had to be very capable by definition. After he'd climbed down, I approached him and said, "You know that kind of work will never end well. You need to stop climbing up ridiculously high poles and start your own business." I guess he took my words to heart, or perhaps I'd found him at a time when he was ready for a change because about a month later we contracted him to work with us on our first project and he was eager to help.

Of course, it wasn't quite as simple as that. Any business relationship will need a little back and forth before a practical working relationship is agreed upon. Initially, his prices were much too high for us, but that was mostly because he had no reference point from which to value his labor as a self-employed contractor. We eventually figured out a mutually agreeable rate. He is now a licensed class-A contractor who can build or fix just about anything, and he is as loyal to us as we are to him. This all happened because I saw a hard-working guy, and presented him with an opportunity to improve his life after recognizing what an asset he could be to us and for others. We were also very patient and understanding with him when drawing up the proposal because it was worth spending the time on making this work, rather than finding ourselves in a never-ending search for the 'right' man for the job.

Another member of our extended family is Jung Kim, our go-to outside lawyer for the last few years. He and his firm cost-effectively and competently handle the detailed foreclosures and evictions we often need to do that would take too much time for Ed to do and distract from his ability to work on bigger, more profit-oriented opportunities. Jung first approached Ed outside a landlord-tenant courtroom after watching Ed win a complex eviction case involving a fake tenant with a fraudulent lease in one of our foreclosure fix-and-flips. Previously, Jung had also seen Ed in his very recognizable power wheelchair at tax lien sales in the same city. Ed easily saved us more than $100,000 in that case that would have been needed to buy out the 'tenant' by subpoenaing an internet firm in Canada to prove the lease had been created online after our foreclosure purchase.

Ed and Jung got to talking about their shared interest and experiences in real estate and tax liens and before they knew it, two hours had flown past. Ed was impressed immediately by Jung's obvious interest in spotting and developing possible clients, the demonstration of a high EQ, and the sort of desire to succeed that is so important but so hard to find. Ed recognized that Jung had the energy and experience to be a possible new team member who could centralize and manage most of our foreclosure and eviction work rather than inefficiently spreading it around various lawyers and firms and wasting Ed's time trying to manage a virtual law firm.

Ed reported back, we all got together over dinner, and we immediately hired Jung. This turned out to be the start of a very fruitful working relationship. It took a while for Jung to learn our ways and for us to learn his, but now he is our go-to outside legal expert to manage foreclosures and evictions. Ed can pop in to look at unusual questions when they arise (like fraudulent leases), but otherwise help us focus on making more money through new deals.

By the way, from Ed's first chat, through to this day, none of us has asked or cared about Jung's schooling or degrees or awards. We like to find and work with good people who have the desire to do well and who perform well on some test matters. Jung now has a lot of work from us because he did what he said he would do every time, he did it timely, and he looks out for things we can improve in our documents and processes without even being asked.

A key takeaway from the origin stories of Maurice and Jung (okay, maybe not quite ready for a Marvel feature film), is that you need to always be on the lookout for opportunities not just to find assets, but also to identify good people. You need to be willing to grow *with* your service providers and recognize talent when you see it. Be patient. No one arrives as the complete polished package. Anyway, it's better to carve a diamond from the stone rather than settle for some pretty, but ultimately less valuable, rock. Our investment in building up a trusting relationship with Maurice early on and Jung much more recently led to highly valued and, in fact, critical members of our team today.

Good people and good workers can be hard to find. So, when you come across someone who possesses all (or at least many) of the qualities you're looking for, it's like hitting the jackpot—don't blow it by failing to cash in on those numbers.

We have had the pleasure of working with many agents over the years, some good, some bad, and some exceptional. Sounds like a Clint Eastwood sequel, right? First and foremost, a good agent is someone passionate about what they do. They are someone who truly loves helping people find their dream home or sell their current property to move on to the next chapter in their life. This passion drives good agents to work hard and put in the long hours required to be successful. They are also highly organized. They know that in this business, every little detail matters, and they don't leave anything to chance. Good agents keep meticulous records, follow up with clients and prospects promptly, and have a system in place for managing their time effectively. If you aren't ticking all of these boxes yourself, make sure your team members are filling in the gaps and dedicate some of your time to personal development. After all, it is never too late to learn these essentials.

Finding a solid all-around team member is tough. It can take years to find or develop the perfect member for your team.

Charlie's Example

Let's look at another example. Early in our real estate investing journey, we focused on purchasing pre-foreclosures. I would pore over the legal notices section of the newspaper, and if I spotted a house worth much more than the foreclosing loan, I would send Sam to the house to place a brochure on its door. Many times, the homeowner would call me. This was due, in part, to Sam's habit of leaving *my* phone number instead of his own! Keep in mind these properties had a foreclosure date in the near future, only a week or two away. When a homeowner called me, I would schedule a face-to-face meeting between Sam, myself, and the homeowner. At this meeting, the most vital piece of information we needed was called a "title bringdown." A title bringdown is basically all of the recorded liens or debts that are on the title of the house. The problem is that we would need this information within twenty-four hours. Title bringdowns are important when constructing pre-foreclosure deals with an owner. Fortunately, we had a relationship with a title attorney who owned a title company, Rick Oppenheim Jr. He provided us with the title of the houses in less than twenty-four hours (unheard of in our business). We closed purchases of many pre-foreclosures in a week or less because of his help. Over time, Rick became a critical member of our team. Rick has provided me with countless lessons on title issues such as probate issues, lien positioning, and other valuable insights! We built such a great relationship with him that we ended up owning a title company as well.

You cannot expect someone to walk through the door on day one and have all the soft skills, industry experience, EQ, IQ, and personal attributes you need to dominate your market. What you need to do is locate their potential and mold them through the way you teach, train, and operate your business. Ask yourself:

- Do you give your team enough space and freedom to learn through trial and error?
- Are you able to absorb a few financial hits so that an individual on your team can fall short before they learn and get better?

If you are not willing to sacrifice a little (or even a little more than a little, but less than a lot) how can you ever expect to have the team member of your dreams? While it is desirable to have someone on your team who has all the attributes that are needed, ***you*** also have to have (or learn) some of these attributes, to teach and guide the members of your team as they grow with your business.

Key Takeaways:

- Identify the team members that you want on your team. We have provided some examples of members but your team will differ depending on your expertise.
- Go through your existing contacts list and see who you can draw on to build your team.
- Go to real estate meet-ups, investor groups, conferences, or speed dating events to meet people also looking to network and be part of a team.
- Do your due diligence—check references and follow recommendations.
- Communicate clearly about your expectations, but be willing to give people a chance as you build a working relationship with them.
- Provide honest feedback. Have the guts to calmly but directly address problems that need fixing and be sure to identify strengths to draw upon.
- Keep in mind when building a team that you might need to provide team members with help or expertise as well. It is a two-way street.

- Giving is a lot more than receiving. We have grown our business and team by giving out loads of free information (see our Basement Tales podcast, website www.cskyfinancial/communications/events, and investment newsletters, among other efforts)

Chapter 5

PERSONAL REAL ESTATE FINANCIAL LITERACY

"The goals you set for yourself and the strategies you choose become your blueprint or plan. Strategies are like recipes: choose the right ingredients, mix them in the correct proportions, and you will always produce the same predictable results: in this case financial success. The success strategies for making/managing money and building wealth are called Money Strategies. By learning to use Money Strategies as a part of your day-to-day life, financial frustration and failure will become a thing of the past."
—Charles J. Givens

In chapter two, we went over one of the steps that will help set you apart by doing a self-assessment before you start your real estate investing career. The first step is to determine your real estate investing level now. Once you know that, you need to figure out what you want to *do* as a real estate investor. Are you going to become a wholesaler (can be done with little or no money and a lot of leg work)? Are you already entering the space as a fix and flip investor (you'll need money or credit, and we will talk about that)? Do you have that and need other connections to value, repair, and sell? Will you be a buy-and-hold investor (residential, commercial)? Will you just jump right to the other forms of residual income investments (maybe you inherited money or simply have enough saved in a retirement fund you want to use)?

This roadmap between levels of real estate engagement has been designed to allow you to enter at any point, depending on your money, position, and real estate investor skill level. Keep in mind: You can do any or all of the above eventually, but I recommend starting with one aspect of an investment strategy, stick to it, execute, and become an expert. We started out in our investment careers being fix-and-flip investors with a small amount of capital. We purchased many flips using the pre-foreclosure method later in the book to build our capital and accelerate our number and size of purchases. The result of doing many flips optimally for each given property resulted in us not just selling and reinvesting the profit but keeping and owning a bunch of residential rentals because that best fit the market and our strategy at the given time and property.

Having learned quite a bit about real estate notes (i.e., loans) to buy, sell, and hold property, we moved down the road to buying distressed notes and selling or holding those because we knew how to foreclose and flip if needed. From there we moved on to more complex instruments like tax lien certificates because we understood by then how to generate passive income directly from their purchase and were knowledgeable enough to dispose of a property in any number of ways if we ended up with it instead of a lien payoff.

I can hear you now. "Well, Charlie, this stuff about real estate investing is all well and good but what if I have no idea of the concept of money? How will you help me?"

You have come to the right chapter. If you are a beginner on the way to personal financial literacy, I'll get you started building your bank of knowledge. If you are already a solid financial pro, you will still learn how to handle money when it comes to real estate investing and how to plan and execute your financial pathway to financial freedom.

What is our definition of financial freedom you might ask? Great question! Let's get started.

FINANCIAL FREEDOM is where your PASSIVE INCOME is the SAME or exceeds your monthly FOOTPRINT. Keep in mind I did not say ACTIVE INCOME.

Let's take a look at a few definitions.

Monthly Footprint = All your monthly expenses (housing, transportation, food, utilities, entertainment, insurance, taxes, etc.)

Active Income = Income you derive from your time-based job in the form of a salary, hourly wage, tips, and/or commissions. Active means you are performing tasks related to your job and getting paid for it. Hopefully, you are making enough money to create at least some residual income to feed your savings. (If not, we've got a way around that through wholesaling we'll discuss later).

Residual Income = Income an individual has left over after living and other basic expenses (monthly footprint) have been met. This is also where you get and grow your savings. Once your basic savings grow high enough to have funds in case of emergency (illness, need to look for a new primary job, etc.), you invest that extra money to create self-sustaining passive income.

Passive Income = Income derived from investment activities where you use your money to generate income. Passive income can provide significant security as it provides steady cash flow not connected to your daily work or time. Passive income ideally is earned with little or no effort. It is earned from an entity where you are not involved, or perhaps only engage in limited effort to watch for problems. Easy ways to passive income include interest from savings accounts or bonds, dividends from stocks, or renting a room in your house (house hacking), to name just a few examples. These are high in ease of investment but may be relatively low in return on investment.

What we are talking about with this book will be how to generate significant and growing passive income from real estate. The goal is to get enough passive income to take care of your monthly footprint, leaving you to work or not as you see fit. Then you will truly be financially free. If you choose to keep working actively, you can effectively double dip with your passive money doing another job for you at the same time, meaning your overall monetary wealth will grow more rapidly.

Now that you understand these concepts, I can put down my pen and stop writing this book since you know how to become free from financial bondage! Maybe not quite yet? Okay, we will continue. Keep in mind we understand there are other forms of passive income outside the real estate world, such as social security income, pension income from a job, income derived from annuities, and such. We are just trying to show how you can become financially independent exclusively through the real estate world.

There is another type of income that pertains to us as real estate investors. Even though we can be financially free, we choose to work to make another type of income every day. We call it self-managed asset income. The name itself defines it as it is the type of income that is generated from assets that you own and manage directly. This drives our day-to-day activities. We are still in a position where our businesses require a lot of attention, and in return, we generate higher returns than even good passive investments. However, if we ever get tired of playing Monopoly, we can turn off the lights on our active efforts and have someone manage our businesses for us. They would earn a fee for taking over our daily activities, and our rate of return might go down as a result. But we have the freedom at literally any time to step away and do anything we want because our passive income so far outstrips our most generous footprint calculations.

Self-managed asset income still can be a form of passive income, but you need some time to manage assets and income streams. What you don't do is simply stick your money in a bank and hope that interest rates and inflation blow in your direction. All of our businesses currently involve asset-based income. We have not set them up yet just to be entirely passive. Even though our money makes money for us we still have an active role in our businesses like managing our investment properties, both commercial and residential, managing our loans, managing our tax lien certificates, etc.

We are still running our businesses. Why bother? For the simple reason that it is still fun. True wealth is not about the number of dollars in your bank account, it is doing what you enjoy doing, which money certainly can help. If and when our business stops being fun because we get old and cranky, we walk. In my case, I will swim directly to Bonaire, Grand Cayman full-time in my scuba gear.

Now that you have a basic concept of the definitions, steps, and pathways to becoming financially free, we need to go over some key financial concepts and how they will relate to your success on your real estate investing journey. As you read through this chapter, remember that the objective is not to rush but rather to help you understand your financial situation better, to make informed financial decisions, and to secure your financial future.

Below are the concepts we will cover:

1. Understanding your Credit
2. Interest Rates
3. How to Build an Income Statement
4. How to Build a Balance Sheet
5. Mortgage Financing
6. Real Estate Equity
7. Leverage
8. CAP Rates
9. Liquidity
10. Arbitrage

Understanding Your Credit

In our journey through the world of real estate investing, understanding credit is vital. It forms the basis of our discussion in this chapter regarding financial literacy. The word "credit" in the financial world refers to a contractual agreement in which a borrower receives a sum of money or something else of value and commits to repaying the lender later, typically with interest. The repayment period and amount are contained in the agreement.

Credit cards are the most obvious example of credit today. Most of us got our first credit card in college or shortly after high school graduation. Maybe you even started with a gas credit card or store card such as Macy's, Target, or Wal-Mart. You kids out there might have an Amazon card.

Credit is also used to describe the financial soundness of an individual or business. Credit is kept in the form of a numeric score, especially for individuals. The higher the score, the safer an individual is in terms of being likely to repay without collection problems. This numeric scoring is a far simpler way of determining relative creditworthiness than, say, requiring and reviewing an individual financial statement and background check that a bank might perform for a big commercial loan.

There are three reporting credit agencies that distill as many factors as possible regarding an individual's creditworthiness down to that single, numeric (FICO) score. FICO stands for Fair Isaac Corporation. FICO pioneered the primary method for calculating credit scores based on information about experience with or regarding any given individual collected by credit reporting agencies. These agencies are Experian, Equifax, and TransUnion. FICO scores are a three-digit summary representation of credit quality with 300 being on the low end and 850 on the high end.

The FICO score is used by over 90 percent of the top lenders because the relative likelihood of default versus repayment can be predicted with sufficient accuracy for the lender to reject or grant credit and/or charge a higher or lower rate of interest to account for relative risk. A credit score is influenced by five categories: Payment History (35 percent), Amounts Owed (30 percent), Length of Credit History (10 percent), New Credit (10 percent), and Credit Mix (10 percent). Credit scores determine a person's ability to borrow money for mortgages, auto loans, and personal loans. They give lenders a simple way to assess the risk in making such loans to the individual being considered.

Credit ratings for companies and businesses are calculated by credit rating agencies such as Dun & Bradstreet, S&P, Global, Moody's, and Fitch Ratings. Often, private consultants are retained to go through books and assets, particularly of private companies, to assess the more complicated credit risk that can lurk in the dark below the shiny surface of a functioning business. Public companies are required to disclose assets, liabilities, and significant risks in public reporting, which investors, lenders, and others can use to determine credit risk.

Why is your credit number and getting credit so important in the real estate world? Credit will determine whether you will get the critical loans you need to participate in this industry such as a mortgage, home equity line of credit, or consumer bank line of credit. These loans are necessary for you as you acquire, repair, sell, hold, or otherwise profit from properties. This is of course unless you already have all the cash you need or want lying around, in which case you should skip to the conclusion section of this book. Also, the ability to get any loan is not the only key consideration. Your credit score will determine the interest rate, which will be significant to your cost of capital (cost to get funds) and, thus, the profit you can make using those funds. Most lenders use the score to bracket the borrower into certain rates. Higher credit scores get you the benefit of lower rates which will then equate to helping your cash flow and rate of profitability.

If you are a person with a low credit score, there are credit counseling services and credit repair agencies that can help you build up your credit score. We understand that one big reason for having a bad credit score is that you are struggling to make ends meet. We get it, and this book can help.

Interest Rates

The next important topic you need to understand is interest rates. The interest rate typically is the amount the lender charges a borrower and is a percentage of the principal (the amount loaned) over time. Interest rates are not only used for loans but also your saving rates, certificates of deposits, or money markets, that are paid to you for your investments.

Simple interest is the most basic form of interest calculation where the interest is charged solely on the original amount, or the principal. Simple interest is easy to understand but rarely used in real-world finance due to its simplicity. Interest rate quotes are usually on an annual basis. This can be the same or different from a measure known as the APR (annual percentage rate). The APR refers to the yearly interest rate that an individual will pay for a loan, including any initial fees. In lending documentation, APR is often the most visible rate because it refers to the amount of interest paid over the year for borrowed money, and often includes some of the transaction costs to get the loan expressed within the total amount of interest cost.

In addition, the Federal Truth in Lending Act requires many lenders to report APR to keep comparisons between loans much simpler and more accurate for the consumer. A 7 percent interest rate to borrow actually might be a lot worse than 6.5 percent with another lender if the first lender has few junk fees and costs while the second lender has relatively higher transaction costs. Getting and comparing the APY from both lenders should help reveal the true costs of borrowing.

Example:

How much simple interest would I pay on $50,000 at 9 percent for the year assuming no principal paydown?

Calculation: $50,000 x 0.09 = $4,500

I would pay $4,500 per year. Easy, right?

Another Example:

If you are an investor in Clear Sky Financial and have an investment of $600,000 paying you 8 percent a year, how much would you receive monthly?

Calculation: $600,000 x 0.08 / 12 = $4,000 a month.

Now, if your monthly footprint was $12,000 a month, how close to financial freedom are you?

Simply $4,000 / $12,000 = 33.33 percent of your way there!

Compounding interest, however, is the more prevalent practice. It determines interest not only based on the initial principal but also on the accumulated interest of previous periods. It can be likened to a snowball rolling downhill, gaining more and more snow (in this case, interest) as it goes. This might not be good if the snowball is a loan you took out rolling toward you but it's really nice when you are on the passive income side of things. Compounding can be calculated daily, monthly, and yearly. Can you guess which method of compounding will grow your investment money faster? If your answer is daily, you are correct!

This brings us to the Rule of 72. It's a simple formula used to determine how long an investment will take to double given a fixed annual rate of interest. By dividing 72 by the annual rate of return, you get the years it takes to double the investment. The Rule of 72 applies to annual compound interest, not simple interest. It is also most accurate for interest rates that fall between 6 percent and 10 percent.

Example

How many years would it take my money to double if I was getting an 8 percent compounded return?

Calculation: 72/8 = 9 years.

So, if you started with $100,000 it would grow to $800,000 in 27 years or $1,600,000 in 36 years.

How to Build a Cash Flow Statement (Income Statement)

Anybody who knows me understands that I am a walking and talking corporation. My personal financial situation is very similar to the way successful businesses are run. I have both an income statement (basically a budgeted amount of income vs. expenses) and a balance sheet at both my personal level and business level. The business income, my distribution, and my salary, basically feed into my personal statements. This is the same way you need to live your financial life. You need to run your household like a business–always trying to increase income and decrease expenses so you have more savings to invest!

A personal cash flow statement measures your income (cash inflows) vs. expenses (cash outflows) to get to your residual income (net cash flow) for a specific period. I like to do this monthly. Creating an income statement starts with creating a budget, which starts as simply as what you might have learned in junior high or what you can probably guess from living life.

Sources of income to include are everything from basic salaries, hourly income, interest from savings accounts, dividends from investments, and any passive or asset-based income from the simple such as passbook savings accounts, CDs, treasury bonds, (and rental properties) to the more complex such as interest from mortgage pooled funds, dividends from REITS or syndications. The expense side should start simple, including housing expenses, utility bills, groceries, car/credit card payments, insurance, transportation, entertainment, or student loans, etc. You should then go on to include the more complex categories you might have or later start, such as fixed monthly investments, rental mortgage payments, estimated investment property repairs, and expenses.

What is left over after deducting expenses from income is hopefully more than zero. Don't panic if it is negative! Keep in mind the fact that you now actually know this, and it is on paper in black and white in an organized way, is a big step on your path to financial freedom. So, take heart in this. Every journey, every marathon starts with a single step. We now have a negative number to use as a start to figure out how to increase income and decrease expenses. Much of this book is about concrete steps to take to fix that, the first of which is knowing where you stand. So, congratulations, you've now taken this critical step.

Developing a positive savings number (residual income) is the key aspect of your income statement. This involves setting aside a portion of your income above expenses to create a safety net for emergencies or to fund future investments. I always say one of the expenses on your sheet should be a line item to pay yourself 10 percent of your income every month to put into emergency or long-term savings.

Next, we will discuss how to build a balance sheet and the relationship between a balance sheet and a cash flow statement. Then, we will take you through a journey to discuss the different maturity levels of an income statement/balance sheet based on our self-assessment of the different levels of investors. We'll go from a nascent income statement of a start-up functioning adult to a beginning investor to a fully mature statement of an established investor. Each has different traits and characteristics that you should know.

How to Build a Balance Sheet

Moving on, let's discuss the balance sheet. It is a second type of personal financial statement that goes hand in hand with your cash flow statement. It provides an overview of a person's wealth or a company's financial condition at a specific moment in time. It consists of assets (what you own), liabilities (what you owe), and net worth, which is the difference between assets and liabilities. The net worth will fluctuate over time as assets and liabilities change.

In basic terms, a house you own is considered an asset, but the mortgage on that house is a liability. Asset examples are checking accounts, savings accounts, money market accounts, certificates of deposit (CDs), house(s), stocks, bonds, or mutual funds. Liability examples are mortgages, car loans, credit cards, personal loans, unpaid taxes, or margin accounts.

Why are income statements and balance sheets so important? There are many reasons. First, they give you a blueprint of where you are (whether you like it or not). This is very important in determining where you need to go and what you need to do. Secondly, banks love this. It shows them that you are organized and prepared. When a bank asks you for your financial statement and you send it by return email that day or the next, they are going to be happy. This goes a long way to demonstrate your competence and to build their trust.

Earlier in the book we had you do a self-assessment of where you are as an investor. Recall the five levels of being an investor:

1. **Kindergarten Investor:** No money and no real estate knowledge, living paycheck to paycheck.
2. **Elementary Investor:** Some real estate education, might own primary residence.
3. **Intermediate Investor:** Have considerable real estate education, own primary residence, and have other investments. Understands how to find good investments.

4. **High-Level Investor:** Real estate is becoming a serious business, maybe five or more flips and owning two or more investment properties. Has a decent team around you.
5. **Pro-Level Investor:** An all-star investor. Highly educated in the real estate domain with a high net worth. Adept at finding deals, navigating marketplaces, and negotiating favorable terms.

Below you are going to find six different sets of income statements and balance sheets. These are all either people that we helped or current investors in our pooled mortgage fund. I have changed some numbers and headings to protect their identities. Hopefully, you will further understand this process and how you can succeed using our pathway. Keep in mind that the income statements are a monthly snapshot in time.

Level One: Kindergarten	Income Statement
INCOME	Monthly
Job (full time 90k/yr)	$7,500
Total Income	**$7,500**
EXPENSES	
Taxes	$1,500
Rent	$2,150
Rent Catch up	$500
Electric Bill	$350
Gas	$50
Water/Sewer (120 qtr)	$40
Car Repair Expenses	$125
Car Insurance	$273
Internet	$75
Food	$1,200
Miscellaneous Expenses	$305
Credit Card Payment	$300
Car Payment	$575
Cell Phone	$125
Student Loans (Deferred)	$0
Emergency Cash 10% paymen	$750
Streaming	$120
Total Expenses	**$6,938**
Residual Income	**$562**

Level One: Kindergarten	Balance Sheet
ASSETS	
Cash	$3,600
Car Value	$13,000
Restricted Stock (26@197.24)	$5,146
Brokerage Cash	$154
401K	$7,800
Total Assets	$29,701
LIABILITIES	
LLC (5 months rent)	$10,500
Car Loan Balance (15.99%)	$17,000
Credit Card Balance (22.97%)	$9,000
Student Loan (Fed Deferred)	$62,000
(Charged off)	
Credit Card ($ 1,400)	$0
Repo #1 ($ 700)	$0
Repo #2 ($ 8,000)	$0
Cell ($ 4,000)	$0
Loan ($26,000)	$0
Total Liabilities	$98,500
Net Worth	-$68,799

This is the simplest example of an income statement and balance sheet. Investo1 only has a full-time job as income. This is active income. Kindergarten investor does not have any passive income (we are going to fix that now that we know it needs to be her goal). Kindergarten investor has normal expenses except she got herself five months behind on rent due to an unexpected health emergency. She is paying herself 10 percent for emergency cash purposes (excellent!) and she has a residual income of $562. Next month the 10 percent and the residual income will transfer to her balance sheet increasing the cash row from $3,600 to $3,600 + $750 + 562 = $4,912. Also, Kindergarten investor would have paid another $500 for rent catch up and the total on her balance sheet would then be $10,500 - $500. Kindergarten investor's net worth will also increase from a deficit of $68,799 to $66,989. Eventually, the car payment and credit card expenses will go away and before you know it this Kindergarten investor will be out of the deficit.

Income Statements / Balance Sheets of Elementary Investor

Level Two: Elementary	Income Statement
INCOME	
Salary ($131,000/year)	$10,917
Rental Property	$2,200
Work Income	$500
Passive Income	$0
Total Income	$13,617
EXPENSES	
Taxes 27.5% (Fed/Soc/State)	$3,002
Rent - House Hack	$600
Mortgage Rental (PITI)	$2,139
Condo Dues	$530
Utilities	$0
Car Loan	$370
Car Insurance	$130
Student Loans (Deferred)	
Gas	$75
Phone	$100
Food/Entertainment/Travel	
Credit Card	
Miscellaneous Expenses	$50
Investor Fund (10% to savings)	$1,092
401k Contribution (matched)	$437
Total Expenses	$8,524
RESIDUAL INCOME	$5,092

Level Two: Elementary Balance Sheet	
ASSETS	
Checking	$20,000.00
Savings	$15,000.00
Rental Property	$305,000.00
Cars	
Car 1	$4,000.00
401K	$40,000.00
Total Assets	$384,000.00
LIABILITIES	
Mortgage	$295,000.00
Credit Card (11%)	$15,000.00
Student Loan	$38,000.00
Car Loan	$7,500.00
Total Liabilities	$355,500.00
NET WORTH	$28,500.00

Elementary investor 2 has a normal salary but also has a job on the side making additional income. Elementary investor does own an investment property (excellent), but it is a negative cash flow from a cash-on-cash standpoint (don't panic, needs attention). He smartly decided to move back in with his parents to allow for an increased savings rate. He is trying to buy a second house from a relative. Stay tuned. The great thing about this income statement is the increase in savings rate. Maybe moving back home was not ideal personally (or maybe the whole family loves it!) but either way, this is allowing him to contribute to his 401K plan at almost $1,000 a month including the company match. In addition, his monthly cash savings will increase by over $6,000 a month ($1,092 + $5,092). Elementary investor will have $72,000 to invest at the end of the year. If he can invest the $72,000 at 6 percent interest this will add $360 to his residual income. Elementary investor will have a net worth of over $100,000 a year from now! Thus, the start of the snowball in a very positive direction. Once elementary investor acquires the second house, I would say he is moving up to the intermediate investor level.

Income Statements / Balance Sheets of Intermediate Investor

Level Three: Intermediate	Income Statement
INCOME	Monthly
Consulting work ($125/hr @ 20	$5,000
Passive Cash Flow Course Sales	$2,000
Pooled Fund ($150M @ 8%)	$1,000
Total Income	$8,000
EXPENSES	
Taxes 20% (Fed/Soc/State)	$1,600
Rent - House Hack	$600
Utilities	$125
Car Repair Expenses	$100
Car Insurance	$100
Student Loans (Paid Off)	$0
Gas	$75
Phone	$100
Credit Card (Food/Fun/Travel)	$1,300
Miscellaneous Expenses	$50
Investment Savings	$500
Total Expenses	$4,550
RESIDUAL INCOME	$3,450

Level Three: Intermediate	Balance Sheet
ASSETS	
Checking	$31,000
Savings	$75,000
Car	$7,500
Stock (1200 @ $130)	$156,000
Pooled Investment	$150,000
401K	$75,000
Total Assets	$494,500
LIABILITIES	
Car Loan	$3,500
Credit Card	$2,500
Student Loan	$0
Total Liabilities	$6,000
NET WORTH	$488,500

You might ask, why does intermediate investor fall into the category of an intermediate investor? I would say because he is making over 65 percent of his expenses in passive income. In this case, this investor is doing a good job of living within a small footprint. Even though intermediate investor does not own any real estate per se, he does have $150,000 invested in a real estate-related pooled mortgage fund. Also, keep in mind intermediate investor is still making a residual income of $3,450 a month while working part-time. This investor is only 30 years old, and surely the envy of a lot of his peers. If he were to work full-time and increase his income while keeping expenses low, the residual income would go up and he would be financially free within a few years provided he makes smart investments. Stay tuned!

Income Statements / Balance Sheets of High-Level Investor

Level Four: High Level Investor	Income Statement
INCOME	
Investment Interest	$6,667
Total Income	$6,667
EXPENSES	
Taxes 22%	$1,467
House Payment	$1,956
Car Payment (Paid off)	$0
Electric - AVG	$180
Gas - AVG	$180
Water/Sewer	$87
Car Repair Expenses	$100
Car Insurance	$286
Cell Phone	$200
Food/Entertainment/Travel	$750
Miscellaneous Expenses	$100
Cable/Internet	$199
Trash	$39
Paypal	$30
Credit Card	$50
Alarm Service	$35
Dental	$36
Life Insurance	$25
Total Expenses	$5,720
RESIDUAL INCOME	$947

Level Four: High Level Investor	Balance Sheet
ASSETS	
Primary House	$450,000
Condo	$325,000
Checking	$11,600
Pooled Investment	$1,000,050
Brokerage Account	$543,000
Total Assets	$2,329,650
LIABILITIES	
Primary House	$275,000
Credit Card	$0
Car loan	$0
Total Liabilities	$275,000
NET WORTH	$2,054,650

This person has limited financial educational knowledge for a high-level investor. However, what this person had and has is the ability to talk to the right people, in this case, a spouse originally and then me. This investor worked very hard at raising and managing the family and had limited time or interest in detailed financial matters. (We all have the things in life we enjoy or need to do, and not everyone loves thinking about financial matters! The important thing is to team up with a spouse or person you trust who has that skill and interest if you do not). Thanks to good family planning and insurance, this person's income statement and balance sheet are now very basic and uncomplicated, which is far from a bad thing.

Income Statements / Balance Sheets of High-Level Investor

Level Four: High Level Investor	Income Statement
INCOME	
Salary (net)	$5,365
Residualized Cash Flow	$0
Property Management Cash Flow	$1,086
Rental 1	$1,950
Rental 2	$3,500
Rental 3	$2,375
Pooled Investment	$1,458
Total Income	$15,734
EXPENSES	
Mortgage Rental 1	$1,367
Mortgage Rental 2	$2,401
Mortgage Rental 3	$1,101
Utilities	$500
Car Expenses	$100
Animals	$1,000
Gas	$200
Credit Card (Food/Entertainment/Tr	$2,000
Miscellaneous Expenses	$350
Total Expenses	$7,652
RESIDUAL INCOME	$8,082

Level Four: High Level Investor	Balance Sheet
ASSETS	
Checking	$3,200
Business Checking	$13,932
Business Savings	$14,495
Vehicles	
Pickup Truck	$24,500
Real Estate	
Primary House	$550,000
Rental 1	$395,000
Rental 2	$799,000
Rental 3	$425,000
Fix and Flip 1	$294,000
Other Investments	
Pooled Investment	$175,000
Retirement	$4,500
Total Assets	$2,698,627
LIABILITIES	
Credit Card 1	$1,500
Credit Card 2	$800
Construction Loan	$0
Rental 1 Mortgage 1	$180,000
Rental 1 Mortgage 2	$6,000
Rental 2 Mortgage	$333,000
Rental 3 Mortgage	$106,000
Primary House 1 Mortgage	$550,000
Fix and Flip 1	$245,000
Total Liabilities	$1,422,300
Net Worth	$1,276,327

High-level investor II has both knowledge and investment experience. This balance sheet was only two years in the making. In two years, this investor did eight flips and accumulated three rentals as well as made a passive investment in our pooled mortgage fund. Not bad! Another thing you will notice on this balance sheet is that this investor is cash-poor and asset-rich. This is normal for any investor who is in total *growth* mode. It is wise to have a lot of your cash invested but you do need some money for a rainy-day fund (six months' worth is one rule of thumb).

In the investor's profile, there is *not* enough cash to sustain a rainy day (even some drizzle) if a tenant does not pay or there is an unexpected layoff. I would want to see the cash position higher, but, overall, what a good balance sheet! Also, the income statement is starting to take shape with the passive income. High-level investor II has some good active income streams. What I love most about this income statement are the diversifications of the income streams: salary (active), property management (active, manages 6 to7 properties), rental income (self-managed asset income), and the investment in the pooled mortgage fund (passive). So, as you can see the snowball is getting its *roll on*.

Income Statements / Balance Sheets of Pro-Level Investor

Level Five: Pro Level Investor	Income Statement
INCOME	
Salary ($300M/year)	$25,000
Rent House 2	$2,400
Rent House 3	$2,000
Rent House 4	$1,800
LLC 2 Interest Income	$11,000
Rentals LLC 1 Partner Share	$10,000
Hard Money LLC 2 Partner Share	$30,000
Tax Lien LLC 3 Partner Share	$5,000
Total Income	$87,200
EXPENSES	
Taxes 42% (Fed/Soc/State)	$36,624
House 1 Mortgage	$2,000
House 2 Mortgage	$1,400
House 2 HELOC	$1,000
House 3 Mortgage	$780
House 4 Mortgage	$950
House 1 HOA	$125
House 2 HOA	$146
House 3 HOA	$100
House 4 HOA	$105
House Maintenance	$1,000
Car Insurance	$250
Electric	$175
Gas	$150
Water/Sewer	$175
Doctor Bills	$100
Car Payment	$1,207
Credit Cards	$1,500
Cell Phones	$250
Cable / Internet	$340
Gym Memberships	$125
Travel	$1,500
Food Entertainment	$2,000
Total Expenses	$52,002
RESIDUAL INCOME	$35,198

Level Five: Pro Level Investor	Balance Sheet
ASSETS	
Bank 1 Cash	$654,590
Bank 1 Money Market	$85,233
Bank 2 Cash - Joint ($8590/2)	$4,295
Pooled Mortgage Fund 1	$1,100,000
Stock Account 1	$1,163,582
Portfolio Program - Deferred	$1,469,817
Portfolio 2 - Deferred	$224,894
LLC 1 401K	$253,362
LLC 2 Pension	$650,000
Artwork	$500,000
Car 1	$65,000
Car 2	$52,000
Car 3	$15,000
Personal Real Estate and Notes	
House 1 - Primary	$950,000
House 2	$425,000
House 3 - Shared ($425,000/2)	$212,500
House 4 - Shared ($370,000/2)	$185,000
Personal Note 1	$5,700
Personal Note 2	$35,910
Car Note 1	$15,387
Car Note 2	$8,758
House 1 First Trust	$170,000
LLC Interests	
LLC 1	$7,500,000
LLC 2	$3,000,000
LLC 3	$2,000,000
Total Assets	**$20,746,028**
LIABILITIES	
House 1 - Primary Mortgage	$358,446
House 1 - HELOC	$0
House 2 - Mortgage	$80,768
House 2 - HELOC	$106,057
House 3 - Mortgage (107069/2)	$53,535
House 4 - Mortgage (86238/2)	$43,119
Car 1	$35,836
Credit Card	$6,709
Artwork	$15,000
Total Liabilities	**$699,470**
NET WORTH	$20,046,558

Drop the mic!!

Mortgage Financing

A mortgage is a type of loan used to purchase real estate. The borrower agrees to pay the lender via a series of payments that are divided into principal and interest and made over time. In most cases, a borrower's credit score, income, and down payment are important. The property serves as collateral to secure the loan. The cost of the mortgage will depend on the category of the loan, the type of loan, the term, and the interest rate.

Here is a little-known fact. Why is it called a mortgage? The word "mortgage" comes from Old English and French meaning "death pledge." This type of loan *dies* when it is either paid off or the borrower defaults. Yikes!

The categories of mortgages consist of fixed-rate mortgages, adjustable-rate mortgages (be careful here), or interest-only (Clear Sky Financial exclusively makes interest-only loans). A fixed-rate mortgage means the interest rate is the same throughout the duration of the loan. The interest rate adjusts on an adjustable-rate mortgage (ARM). I have seen one- year ARMs (not to be confused with your body part), three-year, five-year, and ten-year ARMs. For example, on a three-year ARM the interest rate is fixed for three years then adjusts once every three years. There is another type of mortgage called a reverse mortgage, but we will not go into this. I just wanted to mention it.

Those of us around long enough remember watching the shit show unfold as many were crushed by quickly adjusting ARM loans starting in 2007. Before that, ARMs were a great way to get a much lower interest rate than the prevailing fifteen- or thirty-year locked mortgage rate but they could adjust upward quickly when mortgage rates started rising. In the early 2000s, a lot of people used them to buy homes that would no longer be affordable if mortgage rates went up even a little. Everything was great, until interest rates started rising quickly. The ARMs readjusted upward while people's income stagnated or fell. The technical term for this is "bad news." There is a big cost-to-risk trade-off in mortgages depending on the term, interest rate lock (or not), refinancing rules, or the macroeconomy. This is partly why we are spending so much time on financial instruments. They can be a path to saving and making a lot of money if you understand them and a quick off-ramp to financial disaster if you do not.

Mortgage loans come in various types beyond basic differences in interest rates and terms of years. The two most common types of loans are government-sponsored mortgages and conventional mortgages. The primary government loans are through the Federal Housing Administration (FHA), the Department of Veterans Affairs (VA), and US Department of Agriculture (USDA). A conventional loan is made through a private lender or bank.

The duration of the mortgage or the term of the mortgage is called the amortization rate. You will hear us refer to this as the AM schedule. The most used amortization rates are either thirty years or fifteen years. I have seen some mortgages go out to forty years and some (very few) go to ten years. The longer the AM schedule the more interest you will pay on a loan. Whether or not the interest rate resets or is locked for the entire term is a different but critical issue as noted above.

Other terms that are important to understand, especially for a savvy real estate investor, are LTV, ARV, and LTC. The loan to value (LTV) is a calculation made up of a percentage of the loan amount to the appraised value of the property. The after-repair value (ARV) is the value of a property after it has been fixed up. The ARV can be the same as the appraised value if the house is already fixed up. We need to understand the ARV in the hard money business as it pertains to what the house will be worth fixed up and thus how much we as the lender will be protected by the asset and whether the borrower is properly motivated with the opportunity to profit. The loan to cost (LTC) is the purchase price of the house added to the renovation cost. A hard money lender will lend on a percentage of the LTC provided the LTV of the ARV is within range. The common ranges that we use are 70 percent of the ARV and 90 percent of the LTC–whichever is lower.

There are plenty of fees when originating a mortgage. Some common types of fees are lenders' title insurance, appraisal, document preparation, title review fees, and loan origination fees. Usually, loan origination fees come in terms of points. You might get a quote for a loan at an interest rate and points. What is the point? A point is simply 1 percent of the loan amount. You might get a quote for a $200,000 FHA loan at thirty years, a 6.5 percent interest rate, and 1.5 points. The 1.5 points comes out to be $3,000 (.015 x $200,000). So, your $200,000 loan, which you ultimately must pay back in full with interest calculated on that $200,000 amount, is already down to $197,000 in your pocket before any other transaction costs are considered.

The bottom line is that mortgages are an essential part of the home and investment property buying process for most borrowers who are not sitting on hundreds of thousands of dollars in cash.

Real Estate Equity

Real estate equity is another important term to understand. Real estate equity is the value of the home or property minus any debts (liens) that are owned on the property such as a mortgage. There could be other debts associated with the property in terms of tax liens, judgments, homeowner association liens, or even condo association liens.

Real estate equity is achieved in three ways:

1. The first way is every time you make a mortgage payment, you are paying down some of the principal of the loan.
2. The next wave of value creation is simply appreciation in the housing market. The appreciation of the market is usually done by supply and demand. Inflation also has an input into the market appreciation. (Plus, the macro US economy, local economy, job availability, amount of available housing stock, population growth, and many other factors can affect this). By keeping things simpler and focused on things you can control, you can create more equity by making extra lump sum payments for your loan.

3. Also, the down payment that you put down when purchasing the property adds to the equity.

Understanding your equity positions in your house(s) is vital to helping you along the path of real estate investing. We will talk later in this book about how a simple HELOC (Home Equity Line of Credit) can help you further invest.

QUESTION: How much equity do I have in my house?

My appraised value is $900,000. I have a first mortgage on the house for $350,000 and a HELOC of $400,000 but I only owe $100,000 on it.

ANSWER: $900,000 – ($350,000 + $100,000) = $450,000 in EQUITY.

Leverage

The concept of leverage is critical to your success in the real estate investing world. You must understand the basics of leverage. There are two types of leverage in the business world. The first is people leverage (review the chapter on building your team) and the second type is financial leverage. Financial leverage is using borrowed capital to amplify (increase) the potential returns of an investment. What is the most common form of leverage in real estate? Hint, we just covered it. It's the mortgage! Here is a simple way to understand how leverage works on money.

If I had $30,000 and got a 10 percent return on my money for a year in a real estate investment stock fund, how much did I make on the $30,000? Correct answer: $3,000. Not a bad year!

If I used my money and put a $30,000 down payment on a $300,000 house and the house appreciated 10 percent in one year, how much of a gain would I have?

Correct answer: $30,000.

So, what is the comparative percentage return on my initial $30,000 investment (not including mortgage paydown)? The return is 10 percent in the stock market and 100 percent return on the property investment. Thus, my $30,000 property investment was leveraged by being used to get a mortgage loan to buy a more expensive asset. This comparative return is called a cash-on-cash return. For one investment I used $30,000 cash to earn $3,000 and the other $30,000.

The concept of leverage, the strategic use of debt to achieve a higher return on investment, can be good or bad. It can be in terms of money leverage (using borrowed money) or people leverage (using other people's time and skills). Used correctly, leverage can accelerate wealth creation. But if used recklessly, it can lead to financial ruin. In other words, other complexities with leverage must be considered at all times so you understand the risk/reward balance. There are also different tax and transaction cost considerations between varying real estate as well as other investment options that can raise and lower the potential return. For example, a good part of the tax code extensively favors leveraged real estate over stock or savings accounts because the real estate lobby has been very powerful for decades with the committees in Congress writing the tax code.

In sum, investors use leverage to multiply their buying power in the market. One of the strategies that we use leverage for is to use our credit lines usually in the form of HELOCs to buy housing assets at a 25 to 30 percent discount thus creating more equity. You might wonder how you can do that. Stay tuned!

CAP Rates

CAP rates, or capitalization rates, are the ratio of net operating income (NOI) to property asset value expressed in terms of a percentage. Simply put, the CAP rate is used to calculate the value of income-producing properties, helping investors compare different real estate investments. CAP rates are primarily used in the commercial real estate investing world. It is used to gauge what a commercial property is worth. It is used to indicate the rate of return that is expected to be generated on an investment property. Keep in mind CAP rates pertain to properties that have an existing cash flow. The cash flow can be into the future as well.

Capitalization Rate = Net Operating Income / Current Market Value

The NOI is an income statement (cash flow statement) of the property itself. Hopefully, by now, you know what an income statement is. If not, bookmark the section of this chapter. It is the expected annual income generated by the property. The NOI is the income of the property minus the expenses of the property. CAP rates are usually denoted as 10 CAP, 9 CAP, etc. Cap rates can go higher of course. The higher the CAP rate, the better the deal, if you are buying. For example, a 10 CAP means that you are going to get a 10 percent return on your money. If the property is worth $1,000,000 and the NOI is $100,000, then the property has a 10 CAP. Keep in mind this is a rate of return not considering leverage. The CAP rate is also determined before taking into account tax and transaction costs.

Liquidity

Liquidity is a measure of the money that a person has on hand to invest and meet immediate or short-term obligations. How quickly can you get your hands on your money? In simpler terms, liquidity is the ability to get your money whenever you need it. A $100 bill in your hand could not be more liquid, and a checking account or money market fund would not be far behind by taking out a cashier's check or sending a wire. Stocks can be considered liquid in some ways because you can sell at almost any time, but fluctuations in the market could cost you a lot if liquidated without planning. Also, it could take a few days for the cash from the sale to settle into your bank account. Your home is a relatively illiquid investment. You could sell it and turn the equity into liquid cash, but it would take time to prepare the home for the market, find a buyer, negotiate a contract, sell it, and find somewhere else to live.

It is important to know what your liquidity is so you can move fast on a real estate deal. Some of our best deals are houses that we have purchased in less than a week's time.

How do you calculate your liquidity?

Liquidity = cash on hand (money market, checking, savings) + unused HELOCs + credit card availability (be careful here) + other bank relationships (unsecured) + borrowing power against brokerage accounts + money-raising ability from friends and family.

Storytime: Ed had saved some money from his job as an attorney that he kept in cash to be ready for his entry into residential real estate investing. In 2007, Sam and I gave Ed a lead on a beaten-up townhouse in a good location that was available for $130,000. The owner told us that was the number he needed, he was willing to do a normal thirty-day close but did not want to take the ninety-plus days or go through the hassle and cost needed to find contractors, fix it, and then market it through an agent and incur commission costs. Sam and I knew it could be repaired without too much effort to be worth about $150,000, which was not enough margin for us to fix and flip it. Even better, though, the unfinished walkout basement had the space and layout to add a full bath and bedroom or recreation room that would change the 3-bedroom/2.5-bathroom townhouse to a 4-bedroom/3.5-bathroom including a rentable basement and thus a significant bump in value to about $185,000. Better, but still not so much to be a huge profit for me and Sam given the time involved. But it was a great first project for Ed. Frankly, we already saw Ed as a prospective team member and we were curious if he would have the guts and follow through to pull the trigger and make the deal happen. Lots of people want to do this sort of investing, but not as many can work up the courage to take the leap.

Ed had $50,000 in cash liquidity, perfect credit, and access to his credit union that offered investor loans. Ed put down $40,000 cash to obtain a 70/30 LTV (loan to value) credit union investor loan and set aside the other $10,000 for the basic repairs—primarily paint, carpet, and basic kitchen appliances. Before the purchase, Maurice gave Ed a $20,000 estimate to finish the basement/bath which Ed planned to pay largely from his cash flow as the work progressed.

In just 90 days, Ed used his $50,000 cash liquidity and $20,000 in relatively liquid earnings to get a $185,000 townhouse for just $160,000. Not bad! Even better, Ed quickly got most of his cash liquidity back for the next deal by refinancing the credit union loan based on the new valuation.

But wait, there is more. This was a gleaming townhouse perfect for rent by a big family or multi-family group. Ed rented the property for slightly more than his final credit union mortgage payment, so immediately was cash flow positive but for the needed repair here and there. Over the years as the rent and value went up, Ed took a few cash-out refinances to create more liquidity for other deals while always keeping the rent/repair to mortgage cash flow positive. This property today is worth more than $400,000, but it is still kept in our property holding company as a very easy-to-rent spot.

There are many other ways to generate liquidity, even when you or your friends and family do not have much cash. I will tell you in our funding chapters how I had almost no cash but created the liquidity I needed for my first purchase by making a loan to myself through my credit cards. This obviously, is not a method for the faint-hearted. It's also not recommended to fund a deal that is not an obvious winner. But the lesson here: think broadly when you think about liquidity.

Arbitrage

The last term we will talk about is the concept of arbitrage. This is basically how banks make money! The technical definition of the term is "the simultaneous purchase and sale of the same or similar asset in different markets to profit from tiny differences in the asset's listed price." This is the stock market definition. If a stock price is $25.00 on one market and the same stock is selling for $25.10 at the same time on another stock exchange, the arbitrage is .10 per share.

Keep in mind that I said this is how the banks make money. You are probably asking yourself, "Why would they give me a stock market example? Don't I need an example dealing with banking terminology?" You are correct. The definition of arbitrage that you need to understand is interest rate arbitrage. It is a similar concept. Banks will take deposits from consumers into checking accounts and savings accounts and pay an interest rate of, say 2 percent. Let's assume you also have a government-chartered bank borrowing from the federal government at the same 2 percent. Now, banks give out loans. These loans could be in the form of car loans, mortgages, credit card loans, personal loans, etc. If the average interest rate that a bank charges on their loan is 8 percent, the bank is making an arbitrage of 6 percent.

This past year I coached an U17 college showcase AAU basketball team. I had a player who attended boarding school and was very entrepreneurial. He was always very inquisitive about our various business lines. So, I taught him about our hard money business. One of the problems I would ask him was: If I had $5,000,000 invested in hard money loans at an annual interest rate of 18 percent (we charge 12 percent interest only plus three points, money coming in/out in six months so average annual return of 12+3+3) and I have a blended rate on that money of 8 percent, how much money would we make? Keep in mind that a blended rate is the cost of our investor payouts plus the rate at which we borrow money. If I am borrowing $2,500,000 at 7 percent and I am paying investors 9 percent on the $2,500,000 invested with us then my blended rate on the combined $5,000,000 is 8 percent.

Now, with that explanation, how much money are we making each year just on the arbitration component?

The answer is 18 percent minus 8 percent gives us an arbitrage of 10 percent. Then 10 percent of $5,000,000 is $500,000 per year. Thus, the foundation of how banks, or in this case hard money lenders, make money!

Use the key takeaways below as action steps to put you on the path to building a strong financial position.

Key Takeaways:

- Build good credit.
- Establish your income statement / Maintain (pay yourself first).
- Build your balance sheet / Maintain.
- Understand your liquidity at all times.

- Do your taxes on time.
- Continue to look for ways to increase income and reduce expenses.
- Invest wisely.

Part 2

FINDING DISTRESSED ASSETS

"To pity distress is but human; to relieve it is Godlike"
—Horace Mann

If you've read and followed our roadmap as discussed in the first part of this book, you should have your personal financial house in order, or at least understand where you are now and have a plan. You also should have some short-term goals in mind, such as meeting people in your local real estate community and keeping an eye out for possible team members or independent contractors who have skills you don't have. I assume, since you bought this book, one of your goals will be to find real estate at a low enough price that you can do something with it and profit. The entirety of the second part of this book is about finding such distressed assets.

Finding those assets and making deals is the single *hardest* part of this business. That's because 90 percent of those who fail struggle to find deals, often because they do not have the first idea of how to start. Here's the thing, you need to spend the majority of your time searching for deals. As you grow to be a more experienced investor, you may reach a point where deals come to you, but this is never a given, and hope instead of action is never the way to go.

No doubt you've seen or heard of services that will gladly sell you leads. We won't, they are typically expensive, stale, resold to lots of people, and point to so-called deals that would lose anyone money. Instead of selling you useless leads, we are going to teach you how to generate them and make deals yourself for little or no initial cost. Give a person a fish versus teach a person how to fish and all that.

Everything we talk about we have done successfully ourselves, which means you can do it too. That is why we have been presenting on how to find distressed assets for years now in national (Think Realty) and local presentations/classes (REIAs, brokers, Clear Sky borrowers/clients). That is also why we tell you how to find distressed assets in this book and that you will succeed if you put in the work.

By the way, don't worry yet about having any money to buy anything. The third part of this book is about securing distressed assets after you find them, even if you have zero capital to start. Here, we want you to understand your distressed asset prey and how to chase it down even if you have zero capital to start.

Chapter 6

WHAT IS A DISTRESSED ASSET AND HOW DO I START FINDING THEM?

"Every financial journey starts with a single step; take it."
—Unknown

What is a distressed asset? It's not a Persian rug with moth-eaten corners, nor is it a banknote you left in your pants and ran through the washing machine. A distressed asset is a property that requires a little or a lot of love to repair, or the owner needs or wants to sell fast, or it has significant hidden value you can reveal. In other words, the more problems that drive the purchase price down that are below your cost to fix them the better. Pretty self-explanatory when considered in the context of real estate investment.

A house can become distressed for a variety of reasons. Maybe the owner/occupier is elderly and isn't able to manage it properly, or perhaps the owner/occupier simply cannot afford to pay for refurbishments. Commonly, the homeowner simply cannot afford the mortgage payments and the property is weeks (or days) away from a foreclosure auction. Whatever the reason for the problem, a distressed asset is a property that is not ready to be comfortably or safely purchased and lived in by a retail buyer.

Often, owners of such properties won't want to put them on the market because they are concerned that the poor state will hurt the value and don't have the money, energy, time, and/or know-how to do what is needed to get it ready for a more normal retail sale. We therefore have a property that would benefit from new owners and a healthy investment to bring it to life, but it is stuck in limbo. This is where you can come in like we do.

We can go through the entire selling process with the client in about ten days. You read that right, just ten. However, when a rush is needed, we can do that too. We have purchased houses within twenty-four hours of meeting their owner! By offering the homeowner the potential to close a deal so quickly, relieving them of the burden of repair bills or their financial woes, we are making it easy for them to accept and move on. Rather than anxiously approaching the market with a load of problems resting on their shoulders, they are being given a quick route out of their mess with an almost immediate payout. The point I am making here is that a distressed property will more than likely have a distressed owner so expect to find them in a state of bewilderment and inaction and offer them a fair solution that solves their particular problem. When done correctly, this should be a win-win for everyone.

While considering investing in a distressed asset, there are certain things you need to be looking for to ensure you get optimal value out of it. Firstly, making sure that the property isn't just a cleanup job is important. If the property just needs a few touch-ups with paint and maybe some other interior tweaks, it may not be worth it. This is because your profit comes from adding more value to the property through an upgrade than the value you spent upgrading it. So, if the property only requires superficial refinements, the price you can resell at probably won't differ much from the original purchase price, as a few licks of paint won't transform a property's value (unless you paint it in 18-carat gold). Of course, a property like this still could be valuable to you if the owner needs or wants to sell it quickly, and you can buy it quickly or wholesale the deal to a person who can, and the price is low enough you can effectively arbitrage its retail resale sufficiently to profit despite the transaction costs.

When looking for distressed assets, you especially want to be on the lookout for transformative properties. This is where the biggest value lies. When I say transformative, I mean something like turning a two-bedroom into a four-bedroom or turning an unfinished basement into a walk-out English in-law suite. This enables you to unlock value within the property that wasn't there before. Sometimes, this can be through taking advantage of legal zoning aspects that were skimmed over by the last owners. The trick is to find properties that require renovation when you get them. There is nothing inherently wrong with buying a quick clean-up, simple repair, and resell job, but you'll have more competition and as mentioned already, the profit margin will be much tighter.

On one occasion, I found a distressed property that was going up for foreclosure in a restricted purchase zone. You had to be earning a low income to buy, including through foreclosure. However, upon pulling up the title I noticed it had been released from the program which had deemed it restricted. This meant that now anybody could buy and sell it. So, I went to the auction and I had no competition. Everyone else still assumed it to be restricted and impossible for them to buy because they failed to look at the small print. That was an easy day's work. Ed found the exact same sort of property under the exact same circumstances. Look for unusual circumstances and problems! If you can find, understand, and fix something others cannot, you can get a big leg up and generate a big profit.

Now that we know what a distressed asset is, let's look at what isn't. A lot of people who want to get into the fix-and-flip market think they'll profit from buying a house and making it beautiful even if there was nothing substantially wrong with it in the first place. Watching cable TV shows where they do up a home on a budget gives people a completely inaccurate impression of the industry. They'll go into a property and invest a load of cash installing a top-notch kitchen and bathroom suite and expect to increase the property's value by enough to make a considerable profit. Sadly, this is rarely the result. If the house wasn't a distressed asset to begin with, you aren't going to add much to its resale value by altering the fixtures and fittings. You are simply restyling a property that is already livable.

Others will have seemingly sensible renovation plans that end up failing due to inexperience. For example, you might convert a garage into a bedroom only to find out that zoning restrictions you failed to check render this unlawful–a very costly mistake. Newbies to fixing and flipping tend to spend, spend, spend, assuming extra investment means added value when often this just isn't the case. A two-bedroom property that is deemed livable, won't suddenly reach the value of a four-bedroom property in the same area simply because you've spent thousands on refitting the interior. Ultimately, you still have a two-bedroom property, which could have reasonably housed someone before you splashed all the cash. You don't want to pay for a new high-end kitchen that would look amazing in a million-dollar house when the market for the house you are fixing is $300,000. On the other hand, you better budget for that nice kitchen if you buy a property that is going to compete with other million-dollar houses in the same neighborhood!

So, that's a little on what to avoid. Now for some more productive advice. If you want early-to-long-term success in the industry you need to be marketing directly to motivated sellers to generate leads. The best bit is you can start this without a dollar in savings (all of that will be explained in due course in chapter seven). All the money and industry knowledge in the world isn't worth a cent unless you can find motivated sellers. The best possible approach is to cultivate an informal marketplace that is unique to you (again chapter seven). This will minimize your competition and allow you to find and win deals others cannot.

Here, however, we start with six categories of distressed assets and the relatively easy ways to find them. We still find properties and deals this way, meaning you can too.

1. Pre-foreclosures
2. Foreclosures
3. Bank Owned Properties (REOs/VA homes, HUD homes, USDA homes)
4. Short Sales
5. Estate Sales
6. Tax Lien Properties

Pre-foreclosures

A pre-foreclosure is a house where the owner is behind on their payments to the mortgage company anywhere from three to nine months and has a scheduled court date or auction date. An ad is placed in your local newspaper in the legally required ad section advertising a foreclosure auction date. The ad will have the foreclosing instrument number and most likely the loan amount at the inception of the loan. It will also have the address of the property.

We simply go through an identification process to determine if the house is a pre-foreclosure candidate or a short-sale candidate. If the house is worth more than 70 percent of the loan amount, this is deemed to be a pre-foreclosure. If not, we file it away into our short-sale bucket (more to come on this). Once we have identified the pre-foreclosure, we will either send a letter or postcard (lemmings methodology) or better yet simply drop off a brochure at the house. This type of property is purchased directly from the homeowner. The title is very important as you have to pay off all the liens that are on the property. There will probably be more than just the foreclosing loan instrument, like a second trust, HOA lien, water lien, mechanics' lien, etc., etc.

In most cases, you will need to close on a pre-foreclosure in less than two weeks to beat the auction date and offer relief to the homeowner from the stress they obviously are facing. If you can't close that fast, you can be sure you will have competition with someone who can.

If the property that we identified is a pre-foreclosure candidate and the auction gets canceled then we simply add this property to our pre-foreclosure database and start the marketing process. Our marketing process consists of postcards, yellow letters, email campaigns, phone calls (cold calling), and text messaging.

Below are some examples of pre-foreclosure ads, which came out in the middle of April 2016.

TRUSTEE'S SALE OF

15223 JEANS COURT, WOODBRIDGE, VIRGINIA 22193

COUNTY OF PRINCE WILLIAM In execution of a certain deed of trust dated 12/15/05, in the original principal amount of 485,000.00 recorded in the County of Prince William, Virginia, as as Instrument No. 200601110006024, as amended by an instrument appointing the undersigned as Substitute Trustee, default having occurred in the payment of the Note thereby secured and at the request of the holder, the undersigned Substitute Trustee will offer for sale at public auction in the front of the building housing the Circuit Court of the COUNTY OF PRINCE WILLIAM, VA located at 9311 Lee Avenue, Manassas, Virginia, 20110 on June 9, 2016, at 3.30 PM, the property described in said deed of trust, located at the above address, with improvements thereon and more particularly described as follows: LOT 9, SECTION 1, PLATTED AND RECORDED IN DEED BOOK 2641, AT PAGE 1129 IN PRINCE WILLIAM COUNTY. TERMS OF SALE: Neither the Substitute Trustee nor the holder of the note secured by the deed of trust will deliver possession of the property to the successful bidder.

TRUSTEE'S SALE

9344 China Grove Court Manassas, VA 20110

In execution of the Deed of Trust dated August 25, 2003 and recorded in Instrument 200308290159827, of Prince William County land records, Trustee Services of Virginia, LLC, the appointed Substitute Trustee, will offer for sale at public auction at the front of the Prince William County Circuit Court (9311 Lee Avenue) at Manassas, Virginia on May 4, 2016 at 1.00 PM the property more particularly described in the aforementioned Deed of Trust, located at the above address and briefly identified as follows: LOT 36, SECTION 17A, WELLINGTON, AS THE SAME IS DULY DEDICATED, PLATTED AND RECORDED IN DEED BOOK 2815 AT PAGE 888, AMONG THE LAND RECORDS OF PRINCE WILLIAM COUNTY, VIRGINIA Tax No.: 101-74-00-36 The property and improvements will be sold in "as is" physical condition without warranty of any kind. TERMS OF SALE: A non-refundable bidder's deposit of $12,500.00 or 10% of the sale price, whichever is less, by cashier's or certified check required at time of sale, except for the party secured by the Deed of Trust. Risk of loss is on the purchaser from date and time of auction. Balance of the purchase price must be paid by cashier's check within 14 days from sale date

TRUSTEE'S SALE OF

12612 CRABTREE FALLS DRIVE BRISTOW, VIRGINIA 20136

COUNTY OF PRINCE WILLIAM THIS PROPERTY WILL BE SOLD SUBJECT TO A 120 DAY RIGHT OF REDEMPTION BY THE INTERNAL REVENUE SERVICE.)
In execution of a certain deed of trust dated 08/31/05, in the original principal amount of 575,000.00 recorded in the County of Prince William, Virginia, as as Instrument No. 200509010051253, as amended by an instrument appointing the undersigned as Substitute Trustee, default having occurred in the payment of the Note thereby secured and at the request of the holder, the undersigned Substitute Trustee will offer for sale at public auction in the front of the building housing the Circuit Court of the COUNTY OF PRINCE WILLIAM, VA located at 9311 Lee Avenue, Manassas, Virginia, 20110 on June 9, 2016, at 3:30 PM, the property described in said deed of trust, located at the above address, with improvements thereon and more particularly described as follows: LOT 22, PHASE 2, SECTION 5, PLATTED AND RECORDED AS INSTRUMENT #200401280009215 (PLAT AT #200401280009216), AMONG THE LAND RECORDS OF PRINCE WILLIAM COUNTY. TERMS OF SALE: Neither the Substitute Trustee nor the holder of the note secured by the deed of trust will deliver possession of the property to the successful bidder. The purchaser at the sale will be required to pay all closing costs.

Charlie's Story

One of my daily tasks is to go through all of the trustee sale ads; I check about five publications each day. From these ads, we can identify properties that look like good pre-foreclosure candidates; essentially, properties worth more than what is owed on them. A good rule of thumb is to take the property value and multiply it by 70 percent. If that amount is greater than the loan amount, this is a candidate for your list. The 70 percent rule helps weed out properties that have no equity. The value of 15223 Jeans Court was approximately $425,000 in April of 2016. If you look at the fourth line down in the ad, you will see that the original loan balance on 12/15/2005 was $485,000. If you assume there's a thirty-year mortgage and a normal pay down, the balance will still be too high to keep this as a pre-foreclosure candidate. ($425,000 x 70% = $297,500, which is less than the loan amount of $485,000, so not a clear example)

Now look at the third ad, for 12612 Crabtree Falls; the original loan balance is $575,000, and there is another disconcerting fact–there is a 120-day right of redemption by the IRS. This means that there is an IRS lien, which is a big red flag. When purchasing pre-foreclosures, all liens must be paid off. If you buy a property with an IRS lien, the IRS can redeem the property anytime within the first six months of your ownership. That means that the IRS can come buy the property from you for the price you paid for it. So, you can end up holding it and paying for the holding costs without being able to make any money. With all this in mind, this property is not a good candidate.

Finally, let's look at the middle ad on China Grove. Note that it does not have a loan amount associated with the ad. However, it has the instrument number 20030829; this means that the loan originated on August 29, 2003. This loan is almost twenty years old as of this publishing. Another part of the ad worth considering is the deposit amount, which is $12,500. Given that the deposit amount typically represents 10 percent of the loan amount, we can estimate that the loan balance is $125,000. Since the property had an approximate value of $275,000, after multiplying that by 70 percent, you get $192,500–which is greater than the loan amount, thus it appears to have equity and is a good candidate.

After spotting China Grove in the foreclosure advertisements, I added it to our pre-foreclosure list and then went straight over to the house and taped a brochure to the door (I did try knocking first but they weren't in!) On April 30, 2016, the owner contacted us, and the foreclosure sale date was May 4, 2016. We ended up buying the property shortly thereafter. The seller left with $3,000 and had a smooth transition to another home. We did a $22,000 renovation and resold the property for a nice profit.

Foreclosures

A property becomes a foreclosure at the date/time of the foreclosure auction. This auction has to be advertised to the general public either as a trustee sale or a sheriff's sale depending on your state. Read the ad. Read it again, carefully. Then, read it again, which can be annoying but is necessary despite all of the legalese.

The ad will tell you the auction location, which should be at the local courthouse, the property itself, or at an auction house. The ad says the time the property will be auctioned, which typically is just about any time Monday through Friday between 9:00 a.m. to 5:00 p.m. Critically, the ad will tell you how much of a cashier's check you need to bring to bid on the house. If the required check is $25,000 and you bring $20,000 you probably will not be able to bid.

Another thing you need to know is when you need to close on the purchase after the auction. Often this too is stated in the ad. Some states have a judicial process after the auction where the sales contract you signed at the auction needs to be ratified and approved by a judge. This could take one to three months depending on the jurisdiction. Other jurisdictions do not need this and you need to close in fourteen days or less.

Part of our business model is that we build a daily auction list and use this as our bid sheet. It is important to know what position the loan/lien is that is foreclosing. Senior liens (first mortgages) wipe out all junior liens except for IRS liens. The IRS has a 120-day right of redemption. But if you buy a second trust like a home equity loan, you buy "subject to" which means *you* have to pay the entire first trust which itself could be in default and have incurred a lot of legal fees and penalties!

Two things happen at a foreclosure auction. The bank might take the property back because nobody bids above the minimum amount the bank requires at the auction. Alternatively, the property is sold to the highest third-party bidder above that minimum, usually an investor. In some cases, the second trust might show up and bid to get the property so they are not wiped out by a low bid on the first trust.

Bank-Owned Properties (REOs) /VA Homes/ HUD Homes / USDA Homes

A bank-owned property is a property that has gone through the public auction process and the opening bid was too high for the third-party bidders. When this happens, the bank simply takes the property back. Another way for a bank to take ownership is by a deed instead of foreclosure (DIL). This also has been referred to as "jingle mail ." The owner mails the keys to the house back to the bank. A bank will only accept a DIL provided there are no other liens on the property.

There are many types of bank-owned properties: Portfolio properties, VA (Veterans Administration), Housing and Urban Development

Homes (HUD), United States Department of Agriculture Homes (USDA), Fannie Mae Homes, and Freddie Mac Homes. The last six types of bank-owned properties come from banks that are supported by government or quasi-government-sponsored programs. If the property had an FHA loan and it foreclosed it would become a HUD home. If the property had a VA loan it would become a VA home.

If the bank takes back a property at auction, the bank disposes of the house in one of four ways: 1) Hires a local real estate agent to sell on the MLS; 2) Hires an online auction company to auction it off; 3) Sells the property via a specific website. FHA, VA, and USDA have their own website; or. 4) Sells many properties through a bulk sale process. I have not seen this latter type of sale recently, likely because the volume of foreclosures and thus REOs has been lower than in 2007 and 2008.

Short Sales

A short sale is where the owner sells their property for less than what they owe the bank. The bank has to approve the sale. This is done through a third-party approval letter. The lender normally requires the borrower to submit certain information to the lender such as a hardship letter to explain why they shorted the bank their payoff), two years of tax returns, and current income. Typically, the owner is at least a few months late on their payments and the property must be listed with a real estate agent on the MLS for a certain period before the bank accepts a short sale. There could be more than one loan and other liens. All liens/loans must be addressed and mitigated during the short sale process. Most banks would rather go through a short sale than to foreclose on a house because it limits losses. An REO property sold at a retail market price by the bank is likely to sell for more and at less cost than at a distressed foreclosure auction sight unseen by the bidder.

Estate Sales

This is a property where the owner dies and the property is owned by their estate. The owner dies testate (with a will) or intestate (without a will). When the owner dies, the future property ownership is defined. Without a will, it is a little more complicated to determine ownership and will take time to determine if there are any heirs to the property.

Why is this considered a distressed asset? Many times, people who inherit the property live out of state and they want nothing to do with it and the time and effort it takes to get a real estate broker, fix it up, and wait to sell it retail. Often, they are looking for a quick and easy way to dispose of the property and turn it into cash to be easily distributed to the heirs.

Tax Lien Properties

Property ownership comes with the obligation of paying property taxes as a percentage of the value of the land or house. The property taxes are paid to the local jurisdiction of where the property is located. The payment could be made to a county, city, parish, or some other municipality. These jurisdictions can collect taxes based on their local laws.

Sometimes owners do not pay their property taxes. These jurisdictions can either sell the property at an auction or the jurisdiction can collect the taxes by selling tax lien certificates (more to come later). Either way, they are going to collect their taxes. Once somebody is late paying taxes, usually one year or more, the jurisdiction puts out a public notice of unpaid taxes. This is a great list for marketing your services as a cash buyer! A lot of times these properties are owned free and clear. In some cases, there is a loan specific to the property, but that loan may be a non-escrow loan, meaning that the lender does not reserve money for the taxes due.

Learning and understanding all you can about distressed assets is the key to this business. You need to know how to identify the asset, market to the asset, and create a win-win deal around the asset. Our wealth has been created by simply purchasing undervalued assets and parlaying the equity into either cash or leverage to do other things such as hard money investing, tax lien certificate investing, residential rental portfolio, and commercial real estate.

Key Takeaways:

- Identify and value the upside in a distressed asset opportunity and compare the cost to cure the problems and improve the asset. Ask yourself if an aspect of the property is distressed and if you address it, will it make you more profit than it costs you to fix?

- If you don't know the cost of a problem within the property, then you are unable to properly value that property. Don't invest in assets that you don't fully understand.

Chapter 7

CREATING YOUR OWN MARKETPLACE TO FIND DISTRESSED ASSETS

"It is better to be a big fish in a small pond."
—Unknown

You can find some of the key categories of distressed assets relatively easily. The problem is that the relative simplicity creates more competition for you. Still, you will be surprised how few people actually take the time to look for and act on all of these resources or even know about them. Even though it is simple, it still takes a lot of time and effort to constantly review all of these resources, make target lists, and go after them, so you might be the only one that gets there or you get there first. You can still win and get the deal even if you have competition, though your margins might be lower and your time spent on failed deals higher.

So, how do you minimize this competition and find more unique leads? Create your own marketplace! The best promoter of your business is *you*. You should never stop marketing yourself or your company to generate your market. Our favorite acronym for finding distressed assets is ABM (Always Be Marketing). We really mean always.

If you start out without a nickel to your name, remember that networking is usually free. Call your friends, be active on social media, put yourself at the heart of your community, and get the word out. However, once you get a healthy flow of deals and some cash in your pocket, invest some of those profits in enhancing your marketing methodology. Just, whatever you do, *never* stop marketing.

Here are some ideas to get you started:

1. Door Knocking

Nothing beats personal interaction. Knocking on doors in your community may seem basic but it is still the best way to find real estate deals. All the AI and fancy media in the world can't beat it. I suggest trying random houses in neighborhoods you know and simply asking the person who answers the door if they know anyone who might like to sell their house. That can generate a lead for you that nobody else is going to find online or otherwise. If the person tells you to get lost, smile, and move on, there will be a deal waiting behind one of those doors eventually. You already have the benefit of living in the area and a bit of neighborliness goes a long way to warming up a cold call. You could also leave a personalized, handwritten note at homes that look distressed or that you know are pre-foreclosure.

The point is, you don't have to start with big flashy, and costly marketing. – If anything, this will put people off, especially until you learn how to use paid advertising effectively rather than obnoxiously.

This direct method takes time but no money at all (save for the gas in your car or a new pair of shoes). Plus, the beauty of this technique is that you can do this in your free time while maintaining a full-time job and a family life. All three of us did.

2. Driving for Dollars

Drive around targeted neighborhoods and look for "For Sale by Owner" or "For Rent by Owner" signs. Even better, look for abandoned or poorly maintained properties with grass grown up, a pile of mail on the stoop, colored stickers on doors from the local town or county, or other indicators that no one is living there or the property needs to be fixed and sold. When a property appears to be vacant you can still leave a note. Also, in many jurisdictions, you can look up the name of the property owner and their mailing address if they live elsewhere. Go to the local or county real estate assessment web page, you can often find such ownership and mailing information there.

3. Mailers

Believe it or not, emails, mailing letters, postcards, and handwritten "yellow letters" can be very effective too. This will cost a little money but won't break the bank. You can double up on your door-knocking effort by putting a note through the doors that don't answer. It helps to make the letters feel personalized and to handwrite the envelope. Although we wouldn't expect you to handwrite the contents inside each and every one—you'd be out for weeks with a hand cramp. Draw up lists of properties to target, for example, non-owner-occupied properties (absentee owners), out-of-state owners, those with homes in probate, people who are late on their mortgage but not yet in foreclosure, those who have filed foreclosures, and properties with code violations from the county. We have had the best success purchasing properties after building our own lists. However, a very efficient way to get started is to buy a mailing list from a postcard publishing company. You provide them with the content for the postcard and they provide you with a list of addresses in a given zip code. You can find companies that will help you with lists and mailing if you search for "real estate mailing lists and mailers" in your internet search engine.

4. Leveraging Others

Look out for opportunities for free marketing by attending local events or even hosting your own. You can also benefit from relationships with wholesalers, bird dogs, brokers with "pocket" listings, or even hire a virtual assistant to comb through online listings. Who are these people?

A wholesaler is a person coming to you with a contact already written that they are ready to assign. It might be a good deal, but you need to run the numbers on it to make sure you can be successful with it.

A birddog is a person who is out on the street talking to prospective sellers. Once they find a willing seller they bring you into the picture to close the deal.

A broker with a pocket listing is a broker who is working with a seller who is motivated for a quick sale but might not be interested in having everyone in town trounce through their property and look it over. This type of listing is one where the broker reaches out to known buyers who can close and get the property sold without extensive public marketing.

Finally, we get to a virtual assistant. The virtual assistant is more or less like having a personal assistant except that they are only available online, and on the telephone, as they are usually working from outside the US. The virtual assistant is a great option for saving money on staffing when you first get started.

5. Cold Calling

Cold call the "For Sale by Owner" and "For Rent by Owner" leads you found from driving around or online on Craigslist, Rental.com, 4Sale-byOwner, and online classifieds. Just because you knocked on a door and it wasn't answered doesn't mean there is nothing left to do. Furthermore, a cold call can and should, if possible, be followed by a personal interaction as soon as possible. Unless they told you to jump in a lake, then probably strike them off your list at least until the property appears to be vacant).

6. Online

Having an online presence will be very helpful. You can target a larger audience without all the walking or risk of being hung up on. This could involve posting on public pages on social media sites, writing a blog, or joining real estate investor community websites.

Having a social media page or website gives people a place to look you up where you can put your best foot forward. Perfect for the shyer members of your team with lower EQ!

7. Do Not Follow the Lemmings

Beware of the masses. This is an important message for your real estate business. One of the key factors of success in real estate is separating yourself from your competition. If you are an agent, all the other agents are your competition. If you are an investor, every other investor with a similar strategy is your competition. If you mimic them, you'll blend in and you need to stand out! You must advertise differently, deploy different investment strategies, and, most importantly, you have to keep up with the changing real estate market. You want to be ahead of the pack not following behind and hoping for scraps. Forging our own identity and adapting fast to change has been vital to our success. You can certainly just outwork people, but it is far more effective to work more creatively.

By starting your own marketplace, you can circumvent the cut-throat open market where you'll have twenty to thirty other buyers competing for the same property that you want. When you are looking for hidden gems within a neighborhood, or as Meatloaf would have said, "a Coupe Deville at the bottom of a crackerjack box," the more eyes you have scouting for the prize, the better. With your own marketplace established, you can pay people finder's fees to search out properties for you. Having a wide reach over your search areas will give you the best possible chance of being the first person that sellers approach, whether it be directly, through one of your agents, or by referral for a fee. You must build relationships with potential sellers at the earliest possible opportunity. You want to reach out to sellers before they have been bombarded by umpteen other realtors and become overwhelmed and resistant. Throughout our time in the business, we have found a lot of value in developing our private network. If you are the first at the scene, you're far more likely to get the best price–so keep networking!

Funnily enough, while writing this chapter, I received a call from a woman who found my phone number on our SEO (Site Engine Optimization) website. She called about a property that she'd found in Maryland. By simply answering my phone, I had a lead generated from our marketplace–no driving around or door-knocking necessary. The more your marketplace develops, the more you can sit back and let the leads come to you. If you put in the hours when you start, you'll find this business only gets easier. Of course, I am not really sitting back with my feet on the desk, but I do have more time to focus on other important aspects of the business. For example, I've found the time to write a book!

The other day, I had our multi-tasking office manager, Heather, make a Craigslist ad with our SEO website address and phone number attached. The ad is simple: "We buy any houses all cash." We get a decent number of calls from ads like this. The proposition is tempting, given the alternative of going through realtors and having to wait for a buyer. The promise of cash is attractive to people too.

Another way to build your marketplace is by getting on a wholesaler's list; they'll call you directly anytime they find a new list that would fit your interests. You want to reach out to large wholesalers also, but it will be more beneficial to deal with wholesalers that have small cash-buyer lists. This really opens up your marketplace without the need to get your hands dirty. We also have an email that goes out to realtors every Monday. We keep them up to date with what we are doing and this keeps us fresh in their minds. It often leads to contact with new opportunities. We are essentially making it easy for buyers and sellers to come to us–everybody gets what they are looking for.

There are four main aspects of your business that you should focus on if you want to build your own marketplace:

1. Drive for dollars (aka Hidden market)
2. SEO
3. Place ads on the internet (Craigslist, Facebook, etc.)
4. Build a wholesaler/bird dog team. In its simplest form, a bird dog is someone who works as a freelance property finder–they are willing to drive around neighborhoods looking for distressed assets on your behalf. If they find you a property to sell, they'll take a commission of $5,000 to $10,000. If you want to grow your business, a competent birddog team is essential, as you cannot scale without increasing your capacity to find deals.

When you first find a distressed asset that seems promising (and has owners interested in selling that will allow you to profit from flipping), you need to ask the owner *why* they want to sell. Essentially, you're asking, "What's the problem?" Before you invest, you need to know what makes the asset distressed. If the property is just poorly kept up, it probably won't meet the definition of distressed. If the property is structurally unsound, you may be biting off more than you can chew. You must find the sweet spot you are comfortable with, which will allow you to make a reasonable profit.

Whatever the case, it is always good practice to put the homeowner first. If you can advise them on how to remedy their problems and even enable them to remain in the property (if this is what they desire), then do so. This may seem counterproductive, but it's simply good and ethical business. More than likely, when they do want to sell, they'll be coming straight to you. They will tell their friends about you, and word will get out to someone who does need to sell that you are fair and honest. You don't want a reputation for tricking people into selling or a terrible deal for them–this will kill off your business in the long run. Worse, whatever short-term monetary gain you might extract with a hard sell is not going to let you sleep well at night and have a business you are proud of and want to continue. Before you start creating your marketplace, you need to have a solid plan in place for your financials and where you are going to get your materials. Prices and budgets ebb and flow, so you must do your best to keep within the margins that you have set for yourself. We had a friend who was really bad at this. She believed that by exclusively buying discounted materials from Home Depot, she'd be in the green and guaranteed a profit. Unfortunately, this strategy didn't work. It was nowhere near well-considered enough. Eventually, she was forced to file for bankruptcy. It simply made no sense to buy a property and then hope that Home Depot would have every item on sale that the renovation required. What you are looking for is transformation opportunities, not opportunities to spend all your energy scouring Home Depot for sale-labeled items.

The trick is to learn how to make money upfront from properties. You need a strict budget that lays out how much you set aside to fix deals up. Essentially, you don't want to be freely spending money you can't afford to part with in the hope that your Home Depot-clad house makes a profit, as you may find that it doesn't. If you are making money up front, continue with that pattern repeatedly until your margins are great enough that you can spend more on fixing so that you can sell properties at a greater profit.

The rules that we have provided in this chapter are very important, and they work. What follows is a great example of how our mailer ads worked in our favor. Whenever a house goes into pre-foreclosure, it gets placed in the foreclosure section of the newspaper. The aim is to sell it before foreclosure kicks in. As soon as we see a pre-foreclosure listing in the newspaper, we immediately send a brochure to the property in question. Quite often, auctions are canceled if properties have a lot of equity in them. Nevertheless, we note the details in our database. This allows us to send out mailer ads to properties to remind the owners that we are still interested in their property. On one occasion, we mailed a brochure to the same guy nine or ten times. We could have given up after the second brochure was met with silence, but our persistence paid off. Some months later, we received a call from the guy asking us to make an offer. Straight off the bat, I asked him why he wanted to sell his property to us. His reply was interesting, to say the least, "Well, you guys have been sending me postcards every other month, so I figured if you can afford to send this many postcards you must be able to afford to buy my house." That house ended up being one of our biggest sources of income that year; it was a beautiful home.

Another Charlie Story

Another way we generate business is through something called bandit signs. You have probably seen plenty of those big "WE BUY HOMES FOR CASH" signs in loud colors with sketchy fonts and someone's cell phone written along the bottom. As awful as these signs look, they actually work wonders. I had my son place some around our city on intersection poles, in front of buildings, and anywhere with high foot traffic. Often, these signs only stay up for a day or two, maybe a week if you're lucky. In some jurisdictions, it's technically illegal to place them in densely populated areas. One day my son placed one particular sign in front of the shopping mall entrance, secured deeply in the grass which had just been cut for the last time that season as it was mid-November. This meant the sign had a decent chance of hanging around for a bit. It snowed heavily that winter, with a foot or two in total creating an icy, white barrier around our sign. As the weather warmed our sign defrosted and it had been reasonably well preserved and was ready to work its magic again. Not long after the snow had melted, we received a call from a condo owner based out of Washington, DC. They were based twenty-five miles away and happened to show up at this mall and saw our slightly weather-worn but still functional sign at just the right time. He said that he had aging parents who wanted to dump their condo and move into a smaller place. We ended up buying the place, using it as an office for a couple of years, and then selling it. That was among our first projects in the Washington, DC, market, where we have now sold dozens of properties and have many hard money loans. That sign was the starting point for us, and it was a trooper.

On another occasion, we purchased a note that was not in good standing. It was quite a few payments behind. The house was occupied by a woman who suffered from mental illness and was very unstable. She didn't want to deal with us, but often in cases like that the banks don't want to deal with a difficult borrower and would rather sell their note.

There are several ways that we could have handled this. The most common tactic is to have the home foreclosed and then bring in the sheriff to evict the occupant. However, this would have been traumatizing for the woman. It didn't seem fair. Instead, we contacted her father, who understood the situation. We wanted to try to relieve some of the distress that came with this process by extending the amount of time the homeowner had before she had to vacate her home. We also wanted to connect her with a good mental health facility, so that she could receive the care she needed to get her life back on track.

Ultimately, these efforts proved to be nearly impossible, as she didn't use email and would not answer her phone. The only way she communicated was through long-form streams of texts that I would receive at all hours of the day or night. She'd bombard me with messages that went in every direction imaginable, leaving us with no coherent answers or information to let us act. As a result, we ended up bringing the house to foreclosure at the courthouse steps and eventually took possession of the house because nobody bid on the property. It was a long and difficult process and we had to tread a careful path. Dealing with anyone that is mentally unsound is never an easy process but this was what our marketplace provided us, so we acted responsibly and eventually ended up with the property in our possession.

Key Takeaways

- Market locally, build your own lists of properties, and keep notes.
- Market to your list continuously with different forms of advertising.
- Help people solve their housing problems in general.
- Create a landing page and build SEO around it.
- Advertise on Craigslist and Facebook letting people know you buy properties all cash.
- Create multiple marketing channels to maximize the chances of dealings coming your way.

A Charlie Story About a Pre-Foreclosure

We came across a house about nineteen years ago through a foreclosure listing in the local paper. It had a very low loan amount and the owner had owned it for a long time. I knocked on the front door, ready to recite our whole brochure spiel, but after introducing myself to the woman who answered, I realized she was a friend from high school as was her husband. I also knew her mother, who owned the house they all lived in that was being foreclosed. I was the bearer of some very bad news not known until that very moment. The mother and daughter both had no idea the house was up for foreclosure. It turned out the son-in-law and husband had stopped paying the mortgage nine months before, apparently due to some family drama. It clearly wasn't the right time to make an offer to buy the house since I wasn't talking to the owner. More importantly, the daughter was in shock and needed time to process the reality she faced. I had to get her mom's number and give her a call. I had known the mom for over twenty years! I called the mom and told her what was going on and gave her some guidance on how to stop the sale. I went on my way.

A couple of days later (just one week before the auction of her house) I gave the mother a follow-up call; she was still in total shock. She hadn't known that her son-in-law hadn't been paying the mortgage until I'd turned up at her door the previous week. So, for the owner, everything was still fresh and happening way too fast. All I could do was repeat my advice about the best way to proceed. But I feared it was going in one ear and out the other.

A couple of days later, Sam and I went to see her and asked her how much she'd want for the house as oneoption to stop it from going to auction. I remember sitting in the living room; the house was a complete wreck. Everything was falling down around us and there was a distinct and unappealing smell lingering in the air. This is not an unusual situation when people find themselves seriously distressed.

We all sat bunched together on her sofa and began to discuss a potential purchase price. Sam took the lead in offering $130,000, and his instincts were right. The mom quickly accepted this to avoid the stress of the auction and to receive a cash payment for a property that had become an undesirable living space for her. She might have gotten another $20,000 or even $30,000 out of us, but the daughter and her husband wanted to stay on as tenants. Since I had a personal relationship with both of them and the purchase price gave us some wiggle room, I got Sam to agree to keep them as tenants as long as they kept the rent current. They avoided foreclosure and rented the house back for about three years, and therefore everybody got a good result under the circumstances.

Not long after my friends ended their tenancy, we set our sights on another foreclosure property with owners we could help by using our newly vacant property. This was a nice townhouse nearby, the first house in a decent area of Dale City. Once again, we ended up buying the property, and part of the deal was to rent them the same property where my friends had just moved out. The new tenants set up a payment plan where we took their rent money from the monthly paycheck.

All was going well until about a year into their lease when they contacted us and explained that they were waking up with bites all over their legs. "You mean you have bed bugs?!" This was a surprise to us. We had told them strictly no pets! Jokes aside, we immediately ordered exterminators and asked the tenants to move out temporarily while we exterminated the tiny freeloaders. Little did we know, the house was completely infested.

At first, the exterminators tried a chemical bomb, but there must have been microscopic gas masks, or something because the bedbugs wouldn't budge. Eventually, the exterminators connected a truck-heated fan that covered the front door of the house, and blasted hot air into the house and walls, roasting the bedbugs with 120 degrees of heat. The pest problem was a horribly stressful experience for the renters and for us. But the property investment game always comes with surprises, so you need to develop a cool head to handle whatever comes your way and make sure your pricing model leaves some room for unexpected and unpleasant contingencies.

Looking for a pre-foreclosure is easy because foreclosure sales must be advertised to the public. Ad notices can be found in various publications, usually under the legal section. These will tell you the instrument number of the foreclosing loan, the sale date/time/place, and the deposit amount. Your first job is to determine which houses fit your buying criteria. Once you have found some potential matches, send a letter or postcard, or simply drop off a brochure at the target houses. Pre-foreclosures are purchased directly through the owner, but title and other lien issues still all come into play.

You will need to find out the position of the note that was advertised for foreclosure. Is this a first trust auction or a second trust auction? This is critical to understanding how much equity is in the house. If there is more than one trust, you have to add up the amount of each trust to figure out if the amount of the loans exceeds the value of the property. If that is the case, there won't be any equity for you to pay the seller so it won't be a deal you can make.

You also will need to know the exact amount of payoff for each loan and lien that is on the house. The owner should have plenty of payment demands or foreclosure notices with this information, or you can help them get the information online or by phone. Once you set the ball in motion, you have to be prepared to work every moment until completion as many pre-foreclosure properties will close really fast. We are talking within two to three days!

Although it can be a fast process, remember to tread carefully and act with kindness and empathy as the seller is likely to be in some distress. You are *not* there to bully and to take advantage of people. You need to gather information and find a solution that works for everyone (including you too of course). If there is a cash payment to them as part of the deal above the loan payoff, you certainly can pitch it to them as a win-win situation. Instead of getting nothing from the foreclosure, and nowhere to go, they can have some cash to use to move out or as a downpayment on an apartment.

When purchasing a pre-foreclosure, keep in mind that the amount of cash and the property is not your only concern. There will be a myriad of problems that the seller will need help solving. All pre-foreclosure sellers find themselves at a junction in their lives. For most, the biggest question revolves around where they are going to live. You should be prepared to support them through this transition. We always offer an initial period of post-closing, free rent-back. Once the closing happens, we let the seller stay in the property until they can transition to a new property at a pace that works for them. We build the cost of this rent back into our sales price, so the seller doesn't have to come up with money. To make sure that the seller doesn't decide to stay longer, we have them put money in escrow with the closing agent as a deposit. When they vacate on time, they get their escrow funds back.

Another issue you may encounter is all of the stuff the outgoing owner/residents leave behind. If a house looks distressed from the outside, there's a high chance the inside will be a mess too. You may even need to arrange an estate sale for the seller to get rid of some personal effects and generate some cash for them.

It's also good to have a crew on standby if there's a lot of stuff that needs moving. We build the cost of the house cleanup and move out into the purchase price. That way the seller can leave the house "loaded" if they want to just walk away with a few things while leaving the whole stressful mess in the rearview mirror. A lot of people in these situations mostly want an end to the fear and torment of foreclosure so they can have a clean start. There is nothing like some cash in hand and leaving behind old furniture and clothes for us to take care of for them.

When you are in the business of looking for distressed assets, you have to be prepared for the worst. A few years ago, we came across one of the worst hoarding situations imaginable. There was a whole ecosystem of creatures living inside the same walls with a family of four. We initially spotted this property in the foreclosure section of the newspaper. The family owed $120,000 on a property that was worth roughly $450,000 minus the hoarding, bugs, and disrepair. They were simply unable to address these mounting problems and pay their bills. Their home had been listed in the newspaper for foreclosure about a dozen times. Each time the notice appeared I would go and speak to the owners. However, I never made it beyond a conversation on the front porch.

Roughly six months after my last visit to their property, I received a call from the husband, asking to meet me at a local Starbucks. That next morning, I found myself with a hot coffee in hand, sitting opposite this man, who had his two teenage daughters with him. I'd only just introduced myself when he gave it to me straight, "My wife died ten hours ago, so we need you to buy the house as soon as possible." He went on to explain that his wife had suffered a heart attack, and because she was a particularly large woman and there was so much junk in the house, the paramedics couldn't get to her in time, let alone lift her out of the house to get to the hospital.

"I'm so sorry about your wife," is all I could say.

"You know what killed her? It was the eggplant parmesan that did it," he said. I nearly spat my coffee across the table. A sad situation for sure, but it was hard keeping a poker face. I will never look at eggplant parmesan the same again. It was one of the most unusual yet interesting conversations I have ever had while working in real estate.

"She just wouldn't stop with it, every night she would go out, buy this massive tray of eggplant parmesan, and eat the entire tray in one sitting." I guess at least she died eating what she loved.

Since the property was now proven to be dangerous and, in fact, lethal, the fire department condemned it immediately. The windows were boarded up and no one was allowed to enter. This meant we were now buying the property without any knowledge of what was hidden inside.

We knew the place was going to look like a badly furnished dumpster, but even after hearing the husband's story, we were still not prepared for the scale of the mess we eventually found inside. Tray after tray of mostly demolished eggplant parmesan stacked up high, eggplant parmesan splattered on the walls, and piles of decaying trash. It felt like a crime scene and smelled like one. They hadn't had running water for over two years and they had been filling trash bags and gallon jugs with bodily waste. You couldn't see the floor for piles of trash–it was like nothing I had seen before, nor anything I could imagine. To say the property was unlivable was slightly misleading, as an entire ecosystem had taken residence. At the bottom of the food chain were the bed bugs! Cockroaches fed off the bed bugs and food scraps, mice and rats fed off the cockroaches and black snakes fed off the mice and rats–the circle of life operating under one roof.

It took twenty trucks, over $100,000, and three months to clean and strip the entire house down to its studs. The walls in the duplex were in such a bad state that we were worried about the impact it would have on the neighbors and felt some legal challenges could come our way. To mitigate any risk, we bought the house under a completely separate single-use LLC, so any liability was well away from our main business. Fortunately, as it happened, the house walls were built with cinder block firewalls, creating an adequate barrier between this menagerie and the next property. Anyway, we ended up buying the place for $193,000. After the $100,000 and months of deep-cleaning and a complete refurbishment, we were able to sell it for $463,000. To say this was a distressed asset would be an understatement. This was a very unique challenge, but after buying it at the right price, even after extensive fixing, we made a decent profit. Many would have looked at this property and said, "There's no hope. The house needs demolishing. I can't deal with this mess." Cleaning a property back to its bare bones is relatively simple, if costly. Knowing that this was possible and having the experience and contacts to deliver this paid off and earned us a tidy sum.

Foreclosures

A foreclosure property auction can take place at the property itself, at a local courthouse, or at an auction house. The foreclosure process is specific to the state where the property is located. In the state of Virginia, the owner of the mortgage or deed of trust initiates the auction process through a substitute trustee, while Maryland and D.C. have a judicial process. Usually, auctions are Monday through Friday, usually between 9:00 a.m. and 5:00 p.m. But in Georgia, foreclosure auctions are held statewide on the first Tuesday of every month. So, you need to be aware of which rules and procedures apply in the states where you are operating. Foreclosure auctions are made available to the general public and all foreclosure sales are published via a trustee sale ad or notice of foreclosure. As discussed throughout our examples, foreclosure ads list the time and location of the sale along with the bidder deposit. The bidder deposit needs to be in the form of a cashier's check, money order, or sometimes even cash. Generally speaking, the bidder deposit is 10 percent of the bid amount, but in states like California, the bidder deposit is 100 percent of the bid amount!

When bidding on the courthouse steps all transactions are "*as is* and *where is.*" So, you are at risk of losing your bidder deposit if, for whatever reason, you cannot close. Also, be aware that you are responsible for all rental and/or eviction obligations for occupants in the property, so it is important to know if the occupant is a tenant or the current owner. It is also important to know what loan/lien is foreclosing. Senior liens wipe all junior liens away, except those held by the IRS. The IRS has a 120-day right of redemption if there is an IRS lien. Sometimes, HUD may have a one-year right of redemption as well. After the foreclosure sale, the borrower's right to put the mortgage in good standing may not end. More than half the states have a statutory right of redemption which gives mortgage holders or their successors or others a period in which to pay money and redeem title to the property. Depending on the state, the time period can range from six months to two years! Lastly, county taxes must be brought up to date. Yep, there's a lot to think about. Perhaps put a placeholder on this page–this is the kind of detail you don't want to overlook.

For years, we sent out a "Coming soon" email that let people in the community know what properties we had coming on the market soon. People who liked working with us and liked our products would be on the lookout for our coming soon properties. One of the people on our email list happened to be someone I knew quite well, a recipient of a Hall of Fame Realtor award! I had even done a few deals with her over the years. She had been receiving our emails for about twelve years and was always active when it came to reaching out with a response.

Anyway, in 2022, I was scrolling through the foreclosure listings when I spotted this contact's name and learned that her own property was going to a courthouse auction. Given that we had a pre-existing relationship, I saw this as a potential opportunity, believing that "keys for cash" might be a deal that would interest her. "Keys for cash" is a way to get an occupant of a property you own to leave the house for an exchange of cash (usually $1,000 to $3000). One time we had to pay an occupant $20,000. I digress!

Cutting to the chase, I bought the property on the courthouse steps and put a brochure at the door. A few days later the contact called and we arranged to transfer funds and agreed that she could remain living in the property for a couple of months. Great, a simple transaction with a contact from the past–or so I thought. About two weeks later, I was in a hotel in Virginia Beach, as I was away coaching an AAU Basketball team when I received a call from one of our employees.

"Charlie! the realtor's name on your last foreclosure buy just showed up in a missing person's report in the newspaper."

"What the hell are you talking about? How do they know she's missing?"

It turns out this employee sometimes scrolls through missing person reports as human interest stories. She was surprised as we were, when the name of an industry contact and now foreclosed property owner showed up. Two days later, the police found the realtor/owner sleeping in a car about fifty miles out of town. She had suffered a complete nervous breakdown and her ability to act logically and responsibly had gone out the window. This was sad news, of course, but also presented a problem for us. Thankfully, her family was kind and understanding and supported us as we continued our process. Despite this, we were unable to get any confirmation from the former owner herself that she would honor our agreement, so we had to evict her, even though she had previously agreed to leave. We had worked with the family, but nobody could make a legal decision for her so we ended up asking the courts to help resolve the situation.

Key Takeaways:

- You need a solid attorney on your team that you can rely on through and through. The legal expertise that a good attorney provides is essential and will help you when it comes to contract reviews and more.
- Hone the skill set of being able to develop relationships with people. We saw this in a couple of the stories that we shared in this chapter. When you can create a connection and relationship with your potential seller, it makes the process of a pre-foreclosure much smoother, especially when you operate with empathy, understanding, and willingness to help. Information may give you the opportunity, but relationships enable you to act on it.
- This is an industry in which you need to be able to continue to grow and learn. However, you ultimately have to be doing something of service that's beyond the normal scope. These transactions are not just financial. Look for ways to contribute to the greater good of your community.

Part 3

SHOW ME THE MONEY! BUILDING AND ACTIVELY USING YOUR CAPITAL STACK

"Rod Tidwell: This is what you gonna do for me. You listenin' Jerry?

Jerry Maguire: Yeah, what, what, what can I do for you Rod?

Rod Tidwell: It's a very personal, a very important thing. Hell, it's a family motto. Are you ready, Jerry?

Jerry Maguire: I'm ready

Rod Tidwell: I wanna make sure you are ready. Show me the money. Oh-ho-ho! SHOW! ME! THE! MONEY!"

Tom Cruise and Cuba Gooding Jr. in Jerry Maguire

We promised we would tell you how to buy that distressed asset you found by following our outline in the second part of this book. You have probably been thinking the whole time, "Show me the money!" Well, more than 100 pages or so later you are finally here to learn about all things money.

We are going to start by talking about your need for a "capital stack." What is your capital stack? Read carefully. This is an extremely important stop on the roadmap to your success. Essentially, your capital stack is made up of the sources of funding you have at your disposal to start building your real estate investment portfolio. Whether you have inherited money, stocks, or shares you can sell, or income from other businesses, whatever you can afford to funnel into your investment is the foundation of your capital stack, whether immediately liquid or not.

I can hear you now. "Oh, crap Charlie! I don't have any of this! Have I wasted my time reading all the way here?" Fear not, if you're starting from scratch, the journey is still very doable; you'll just need a little more patience. Maybe you'll have to wait for your least favorite aunt to die and leave you a healthy sum (kidding!). Perhaps you have some assets you can sell at auction, or it could mean a trip to the bank to work out your credit capacity, whatever it is you can make this work. I promise. The bottom line is that once you have spendable cash or credit, you've got a stack. But if you struggle to get that stack, or are starting from zero, read carefully. Make sure not to forget the wholesaling option we go over in detail; that doesn't require any capital at all to generate your capital stack.

So, how much capital do you need in your stack?

You're aiming for $50,000 in your capital stack, and you want to get there fast. We believe that is the amount you need in reserve before you can begin real estate investing in earnest. If you are a skilled investor, then you might be able to generate cash by flipping a couple of properties with just that $50,000 to start and use the profit to grow your stack for more purchases.

There are ways to get around our capital stack requirement if you do not have $50,000 right now. We discussed wholesaling, which you can start with zero capital and then use the profits to build your first $50,000 stack. We even talked about house sharing and other methods to lower your expenses and quickly generate savings.

Another possibility is to approach hard money lenders, and we'll talk a lot about hard money borrowing. Here's how it might go if you come to us without any money:

You: "Hey, how much would you lend me to get going on this asset I can sell for $300,000?"

We might say: "If you put down your $50,000, we can lend you another $150,000."

If you do that transaction with us, you can spend up to $200,000 on acquisition and renovation. You're ready to go–if you come to us already having $50,000.

Now, you may find such a good deal that a hard money lender would loan you all of the purchase and renovation costs. Let's say you got the deal we just discussed for a total purchase price of $125,000 plus $50,000 in expected renovations. We or another hard money lender might loan you 100 percent of the $175,000 because there is so much equity to protect the loan. We have a real-life story below on how this happened for one deal we loaned.

That said we really would rather you have skin in the game. We want you to have the incentive to do the work and profit because your own $50,000 or so is on the line. We want you to succeed because we then profit and it saves us the time and disruption of having to foreclose and complete the project, even if there is plenty of equity to do so.

You also may have more creative ways to access capital than you think. We have a whole chapter on that coming up, including a story about how I generated my capital stack from a standing start to fund my first purchase.

Chapter 8

WHOLESALING TO MAKE MONEY

"Without hard work, nothing grows but weeds."
—Gordon B. Hinckley

"We might describe our world as having retail sanity, but wholesale madness."
—Peter Thiel

Wholesaling is a great way to start building your capital stack without the need for cash, credit, or the advanced skills that we also cover in this book. Let's start by digging into exactly what wholesaling is. Put simply, if you can find a lead and make a deal by putting the house under contract, you can sell (assign the contract) that deal to someone who has the money to execute it even if you don't have a pot to piss in. A critical part of this is that the buyer's name (presumably yours) must have an "AND/OR ASSIGNS" clause next to it.

Yes, you read that correctly, you can enter deals and make money on real estate investing without a nickel or dime to your name by assigning the contract in return for a fee. More good news—if you have found a few good deals and have made contacts and gotten some experience, it shouldn't be too difficult for you to generate some hard money or similar financing to do the deal yourself instead of wholesaling.

The only downside is that wholesaling isn't always that exciting and you might be leaving some money on the table. It doesn't offer all the whistles, bells, and excitement of fixing and flipping, nor the possibility of capturing more of the profit for yourself. But that will come in good time once you have some capital and skills under your belt. This is why patience is a must. Keep focused on that shiny prize and you'll get through the boring bits before too long.

Wholesaling is pretty simple: You find an opportunity and you sell that opportunity to someone else. Of course, it is a shame to pass on the opportunity yourself, but you are probably at a stage in your business development where you cannot execute the deal effectively. You will gain a valuable learning experience which will help you when it's your time to take on the challenge. You'll be selling the opportunity for a smaller share of the possible profit from the property, as quickly as possible, which will allow you to make money in as little as three weeks. You might only make a few thousand on your first deal, but as you get better at these deals (practice makes perfect), you'll find that number steadily increases and you can make as much as $50,000 per wholesale deal. This is not a pie-in-the-sky pipe dream we are trying to sell you here. This is a reality we can vouch for.

Recently, a wholesaler brought us a deal that ultimately landed us a cool $74,000 while the wholesaler took away a tasty $42,000. We met this wholesaler at a meetup. The wholesaler brought us a deal on 4336 Polk Street in Washington, DC. We ended up buying this property for $115,000. The after-repair value (ARV) on the property was $300,000. This was an unbelievable buy with a lot of profit margin for us. The property was tiny. It was a semi-detached duplex unit with only 800 square feet. It had two bedrooms, one full bath, and one and a half bath. It also came with a hole in the roof–not something this wholesaler had the money or experience to tackle. The property had been sitting vacant for a year or so. Keep in mind we did not know at the time how much the wholesaler was making but did not care. We ended up spending $83,000 on the renovation as it needed a full gut. We fixed and flipped the property in less than eight months. This suited us fine, as we reached our return, which was about 35 percent of the sale price of that property. It's not easy money, mind you, we worked our asses off for our fee. We ended up with the bigger pot but the wholesaler worked smart, not hard, getting all their work done in a week by assigning the deal to us and making a handsome profit in the bargain. Remember how we keep harping on teams? This was a one-off combination where we added our skills to those of the wholesaler to make this deal profitable for everyone.

It is not uncommon for "wholesale" purchasers to get good at finding and closing deals before they can expertly fix and flip a property. If you find a deal that a flipper thinks they can profit $50,000 on they'll often be more than happy to pay $5,000 to $10,000 for the pleasure of doing just that. As long as the deal is good, there should be plenty of money to share around and that's really all investors will need to know to get interested.

So, Sam, where's the small print when it comes to wholesaling? What's the catch? Well, to wholesale well, you need to be able to find a deal that is ultimately profitable. Once you find a profitable deal, there are many ways you can extract some or all of that profit for yourself. The crucial question is , "How do you recognize a profitable deal?" Imagine if we had agreed to pay $220,000 to buy the Polk property and paid the wholesaler fee. After our renovation costs, we would have lost money. If the wholesaler entered the Polk deal for $200,000 with the hope of making $20,000, they would be out of luck because there still would be insufficient profit for us to buy at that price at all, much less pay the wholesaler anything.

Know Your Numbers

Whether you're wholesaling or fixing/flipping, you will need to know your numbers and how to generate them. The basic numbers consist of ARV, renovation costs, buying closing costs, selling closing costs, and holding costs.

After Repair Value (ARV)

The ARV is simply the value of the property after it has been renovated to move-in condition. A renovation can involve anything from new carpets and a splash of paint to a full gut and refurbishment; this is dependent on the condition of the property as you found it versus the baseline condition that is normal in the relevant retail market. The ARV represents the current market value of the property within three months; this is because it is impossible to predict longer-term changes in the market that will affect the property's value. You still remain at some risk of sudden, harder-to-anticipate 'black swan' market disruptions such as COVID-19, but generally, a market should not shift too significantly over ninety days.

You can get a good sense of the ultimate sale price and condition by looking at homes for sale in your target neighborhood(s), either online or in person. We use the MLS (Multiple Listing Service) to generate our ARVs. In most states, you need to be a licensed agent to have access. Look for sales of a similar asset class at the subdivision level for accurate sales data. If the property is rural in nature, it might be harder to comp. If you do not have access to the MLS, going to real estate meetups or investment groups and building a Rolodex of investor-friendly real estate agents is a must if you want to be able to estimate sale prices accurately.

Building healthy relationships with people buying wholesale may present you with the opportunity to mine free information. For example, "Hey John, how are the kids, good? Yeah, just calling to ask you if you have any idea what a three-bedroom, two-bathroom townhouse in Silverlake would be worth in retail?" You know that kind of thing–free expertise through knowing someone who knows. After checking in with a few of these contacts, let's say four or five, if their estimates are roughly the same, you should have a pretty good idea of the market value.

Renovation Costs

This is a variable cost that you'd ideally iron out with a contractor before the start of a job. Essentially, you want to make sure that there are no cost overruns that will eat away at your profits. Renovation costs cover the building materials and labor that go into the renovation of a property. It's very important to find a good contractor who can generate a budget and stick to it. Most contractors will factor in a 10 percent cost overrun. Although this means you are paying a little more, this keeps the cost as static as possible rather than finding costs spiraling out of control as the project unfolds, blowing apart your initial budget, and ruining your profit margins. Again, you can probably get some good estimates from contacts—ask for pictures of the inside of the house (although be wary of anyone who might want to steal your deal). Other things to keep in mind—-does the house need windows, HVAC, siding, roof repair, new plumbing, or electrical wiring? If overlooked, these are common areas that could end up spoiling your deal through unexpected expenses. Also evaluate the age and appearance of a property to consider whether it might have relatively hidden defects like a bad foundation, FRT plywood, plastic water lines instead of copper, asbestos, lead paint, mold, or other potentially expensive problems. A good contractor will know how to look for those sorts of problems, and over time you will as well.

Buyer Closing Costs

These are the typical expenses that come with buying a property. These costs are static in nature (our favorite kind), so you'll know the costs going into the transaction. These costs might include loan costs, inspections, recording fees, title company fees (lender's/owner's title insurance, title abstracts, etc.), attorney fees, taxes, insurance (hazard), wholesaler fees, wire fees, and courier fees.

Holding Costs

Holding expenses accumulate during the fix/flip process. Wholesalers need to understand these costs because they can dramatically influence the profitability of the project. These are variable costs that drive the profitability of the project. The holding costs include ongoing expenses such as flip loan repayment (typically interest only), property taxes, insurance, utilities, or HOA/condo dues. Keep in mind that the quicker you can execute a flip after you've fixed up the property, the lower the holding costs you'll need to pay and the higher the profit.

Seller Closing Costs

These too are fixed in nature and are the expenses associated with selling the property. These costs include realtor fees, title fees, attorney fees, transfer fees, and buyer subsidy fees. These costs are fairly standard so just make sure you understand these costs before entering into a purchase.

Finding a Cash Buyer for Your Wholesale Deal

Now let's look at where you are going to find cash buyers to wholesale your deal. There are three primary ways to find them:

1.) Whenever a house goes into foreclosure, a public ad is put in the newspaper. Note the date and time of that ad, show up on the courthouse steps in your town along with all the other bidders, and introduce yourself. "Would you like some of my deals? Great! I'll email a wholesale package!" It's that simple, you've just found an entire market of buyers who will be just as happy to buy your profitable deal as buying a good deal through foreclosure.

2.) As mentioned already, there are real estate investment groups or meetups in every city across America. Find them online, show up, and introduce yourself as a wholesaler. You'll meet fix and flippers, and you'll exchange names and details before you know it.

3.) Buy a list of cash buyers or go through MLS (Multiple Listing Service) and search for cash buyers and/or courthouses. The only thing to watch out for here is that you ideally want cash buyers who have bought several properties already, not the occasional inexperienced buyers.

Practical Wholesaling Scenario

Now let's look at a practical example of wholesaling. Let's say there is a house in the suburbs of Manassas, Virginia. It's a single-family home. The house will be worth approximately $300,000 when it is fixed up, depending upon the neighborhood, of course. But it needs a ton of work; it's dilapidated and not ready to be a new home for a typical family.

We might offer the owner $200,000 for this house given the amount of work needed to bring it back to life. If the owner agrees, we will aim to close within two weeks, paying in cash. The next step is to take the $200,000 contract to Mr. Fix and Flip Investor, he's the best fix-and-flip investor around. I'll sell him my contract for $25,000. So, in essence, he is going to buy that house for $225,000 in cash, within two weeks. I'm assigning the contract for $25,000 and the owner is getting $200,000. As a wholesaler, I just made $25,000, but I didn't put any of my own money into the property. The flipper takes all of the risks and costs from there of the property, including purchase, repair, and resale or rental. As the wholesaler, you never take ownership of the house (hence the term wholesaling) and you walk away with the agreed fee in your bank account. So, there you have it: your opportunity to invest in real estate with only time and effort as your starting capital!

Let's review these critical steps in the wholesaling process as we bring this chapter to a close:

1. Find the deal.
2. Negotiate with the seller and put the house under a simple contract allowing "assigns."
3. Be sure to use the clause AND/OR ASSIGNS next to the buyer's name so this makes the contract assignable.
4. Get a cash buyer for the house. This needs to be a buyer that can close within the terms of the contract.
5. Have the buyer execute a contract assignment (should be one or two pages at the most).
6. Arrange the closing through a title company and close the deal.

Key Takeaways:

- Build your cash buyer list.
- Understand how to find distressed assets.
- Market to those owners.
- Find out what is beneath the rejections you are getting, then dig deeper to tweak and reframe your offer in the future.
- Build community relationships.
- Build your wholesale package.

Chapter 9

YOU MIGHT ALREADY HAVE MORE MONEY THAN YOU THINK

"I decided to see every problem as an opportunity to find a solution."
—Walt Disney

I did not have much money saved when I decided to start real estate investing. What to do? There are many creative ways to raise capital. We talked early in this book about reducing your expenses as a method to save money more rapidly, such as by house sharing, reducing discretionary spending, and so on. Having friends and family with a high net worth they are willing to loan you also is great.

Here is the way I found the money to do my very first real estate investment.

Charlie's Story

My first distressed asset purchase was an *all-cash* purchase in 2002. At the time, I had a good tech job and great credit but no cash. I had recently separated from my spouse, had two kids, and wanted another house to live in. Over the years, I built up a bunch of Visa and MasterCard gold cards, which allowed you to go into the bank and withdraw cash. However, this came with a 3 percent cash advance fee and a high-interest rate. I had between ten and fifteen different accounts with between $10,000 and $25,000 of credit on each card. I was an armchair investor and kept track of my credit with the hope of investing in a distressed property. I also had acquired some industry knowledge but had no deals under my belt.

I was going from one trustee sale ad (where a house is scheduled to be foreclosed on at the courthouse steps) to another when eventually I stumbled upon a 1998 townhouse that had a lot of equity. The ARV (remember, that's after repair value) on the townhouse was $220,000, and the foreclosing loan amount was about $145,000. At only four years old, the property was still occupied by the original owner. To cut a long story short, I negotiated a purchase price of $165,000, but I had to close in under two weeks because of the auction date. The owner was a schoolteacher and had been planning on moving out of state once the school year was over. So, off I went to the bank with all my cards and put $165,000 into my checking account! I managed to close on the house. That meant I owned a property worth $220,000 free and clear. I then refinanced the house with a traditional mortgage and paid off my credit cards. Once the property started increasing in value, I attached a home equity line of credit (HELOC) for future liquidity. Simple. I still own this property to this day.

Access to cash increases as your skill in investing increases. If you have not already figured it out, cash does not necessarily mean green bills piled under your bed. It means the ability to raise funds for a particular deal. As beginner investors, you may not have much cash at your disposal but as you gain more experience, your tranches of cash and/or your ability to pull more cash from credit lines will increase. This leads us to the matter of liquidity (get the mop). *Liquidity* is the measure of money that a person has available to invest and meet immediate or short-term obligations. How much cash can you get and how quickly can you get it? You need to know what your liquidity is so you can move quickly on a deal (before it dries up). Below is a simple formula on how to calculate liquidity:

Liquidity = cash on hand (money market, checking, savings) + unused HELOCS + credit card availability (be careful here) + other bank relationships (unsecured) + borrowing power against brokerage accounts + money-raising ability from friends, etc.!

Chapter 10

BORROWING TO MAKE MONEY

"I would borrow money all day long
if the cost of borrowing is less than the expected return"
—Brad Schneider

There are many different ways to borrow money to make money, sometimes even if you have little or no cash to start. The key is not so much the cost of borrowing but rather the net return. Consider my story about using credit card cash advances for my first purchase. That cost me a lot of fees and a high interest rate but the net return I expected was still very high after factoring that and the risk into my decision-making process.

Let's say you found a great property with lots of equity after repairs and you are ready to move beyond wholesaling to fix and sell it yourself, perhaps because you are a contractor or have a good one on your team. Let's also say you still have very little cash. The equity in that good deal might be all you need to borrow most or all of the purchase money. "How could that be?" you ask. Let me show you by telling you our story of becoming lenders.

In 2012, we were in a great position to do something else in the real estate investing business. We had flipped over 200 houses and had a residential rental portfolio of about 30. We had some cash lying around burning a hole in our pockets. Sam hates it when I say this because he knows in the near future, I will spend it. I had been attending courthouse auctions for about four years straight, never missing an auction in Prince William County, VA. Attending auctions for that long, you get to know the bidders and they end up becoming your friends (not even thinking that they will become clients in the future). You talk during downtime getting to know them and their families.

During this time a group of new bidders started showing up at the auction block and totally decimated the flip profit margins. It was obvious to us that the foreclosure way of buying properties was starting to dry up because of this new competition.

A fellow bidder and friend, Jimmy Hunyh, approached me one morning at an auction and said "I just bought a condo today at the Fairfax County auction for $225,000. It is worth $350,000 and you will lend me $225,000. It does not need much work." Well, I thought to myself, if I was at the auction and had a chance to buy a condo worth $350,000 for $225,000, would I do it? Yes, in a New York minute. So, I said Jimmy, I will loan you $225,000 to be in the First Trust Position. The loan was asset-based and our risk was covered by the after-repair value of the asset. If Jimmy somehow messed up the renovation or some unexpected disaster arose, my loan would be protected by that equity. I could just foreclose and finish the project.

Now, I had no clue what I was doing, but later that night I asked Jimmy to send me the contract and I sent him a one-page term sheet defining the loan. Meanwhile, Sam was working to get our first set of loan documents together (promissory note, deed of trust, etc.). Thus, the start of our entrance into the hard money business and our lesson via Jimmy that you can access capital when you have a deal with a strong equity position even if you are starting with little cash.

Remember the most important part of real estate investing is finding the assets. The next important part is finding the money. Believe it or not, most people fail to enter the business because of their fear of not having enough money. This should probably be included in the first chapter as to why people fail in this business! When we started buying pre-foreclosures in 2003, the term "hard money" did not even exist.

There are many other borrowing and money sources in the residential investing business. The sources listed here are in no particular order and we will discuss each below:

- cash (liquidity)
- soft money (community banks)
- hard money (asset-based lending),
- traditional mortgages (VA/FHA can be assumable)
- owner financing
- subject to the existing mortgage (subject to's)
- debt service coverage ratio loans (for buy and hold investors)
- home equity line(s) of credit (HELOC)

Cash

We need to mention cash because as you get more mature in your investment career you will have some money on the sideline. You might even have enough to close a real estate deal! This is the easiest form of financing, if you can call it that, and allows you to close deals quickly. Basically, you are borrowing from yourself. You figure that a fix and flip deal is going to make you more of a return on your cash than the stock market or some alternative investment. What you give up by using your cash is called the "opportunity cost." I might make 7 percent annually on average in the stock market with volatility but assume lower long-term risk while I might make 20 percent profit on my cash in 180 days via a real estate deal with more risk. My opportunity cost is about 3.5 percent (half a year at 7 percent) so my net return after opportunity cost would be 16.5 percent.

Our best deals have come by closing a property in forty-eight hours or less because of our cash availability and credit lines (liquidity). The biggest disadvantage to cash is scalability and a non-leveraged return. If you aren't borrowing money, you are not taking advantage of leverage. That means you can't buy as much or make an arbitrage return on top of your borrowing rate by borrowing lower than the return you are receiving. In addition, if you use all your cash on non-leveraged returns your potential ROI(return on investment) is reduced.

Soft Money

The next option is borrowing from someone else via a soft money or hard money loan. So, what is the difference between soft money and hard money? Let's start with soft money. It is primarily run by the community banks in your area. Most often, a community bank is a bank that is identified as having $1 billion in assets or less. However, some community banks can have assets up to $2 billion. Generally, these banks lend in only one state or smaller areas and have between zero and five branches. Community banking is the old way that savings and loans used to work. The bank provides a few options for savings and loans in your area, but the offering is local and might not be the same in other areas. When giving a loan, the bank considers both the asset and you as an individual borrower.

All of these things are part of the sometimes lengthy qualification process—they're going to pull credit on you, they're going to check your tax returns, and they're going to request to see your business tax returns, income statements, and a lot more documentation. They'll also want to know that the asset is going to stand financially on its own. Community banks require about a 20 to 25 percent down payment on their loans. The types of products they have are fix and flip lines, buy and hold lines, and hard money lines (very rare). These loans are primarily commercial loans and the interest rates tend to fluctuate.

Hard Money

Now, what is hard money and what are its benefits compared to soft money? Hard money is what we do at Clear Sky Financial. The term "hard money," sometimes called "private lending," refers to hard asset lending. This is where a lender lends money but the only qualification is the asset that they're lending on. There's no other documentation required. Literally. There's no application, no pulling of credit, no checking on income or taxes—none of that. The harder the money, the more it's asset-only and faster. Whereas the softer the funding, the more underwriting requirements on the loan as it is no longer entirely asset-based lending.

Some lenders call themselves hard money lenders just to charge higher interest rates. But don't be fooled: they are not because they require quite a bit of documentation. With softer money, you have more time to go through the lending/underwriting process, and with that, you get a better interest rate. While softer money takes longer, the upside is you are getting a better interest rate that (as of this writing) tends to sit between 4 percent and 7 percent. On the flip side, harder money is much faster and has a higher interest rate, anywhere between 10 percent and 15 percent. The reason why the community bank's interest rate is so much lower is because their measured risk of your potential default is lower than the other less documented loans. Plus, with a community bank loan, if you default very soon after origination the asset might not cover everything. But they'll take that risk because they've looked at your credit, your prior business history, and everything else. Not to mention, you put down a larger down payment with a community bank loan than you will with a hard money loan!

Loan Sharks (A Bad Form of Hard Money)

Loan sharks do not exist in soft money, of course. Loan sharks charge a really high interest rate and if you don't pay them back, they don't just foreclose on you, they break your kneecaps. We do not recommend that method of raising capital! Hard money charges high rates but nobody breaks your legs if you default. In fact, hard money lenders often require recourse for default only against the property securing it and not your personal funds. Of course, some hard money lenders will demand recourse against your assets so be careful you understand the agreement you are signing!

Hard money is always going to be the most expensive loan product. The lender is taking a big risk based just on the project's equity and little else. However, people are willing to pay those high rates to get the typically fast speed of such lenders and not have their personal space inspected by credit checks, background checks, or employment and income documentation.

As a hard money lender, we do care about credit if we know the borrower is going to rely on their credit to exit our loan into a buy-and-hold loan. However, most times we are just giving fix and flip loans and the borrower's credit doesn't come into play. That's because while they're buying a property with our money and using our money to renovate it, fix it, put it on the market, and sell it, we ultimately get paid back fairly quickly. They can do all of this within a few months because a hard money loan can move much faster. This explains why when somebody's trying to buy something quickly, it's just impossible to get the financing through a regular bank.

We sometimes do something almost impossible with soft money, which is we finance a purchase within twenty-four hours. All we need is the title search to be completed and a chance to review the title binder and we are good to go.

Simply put, speed and simplicity are unheard of when dealing with soft money or any other loan type outside of hard money. There's a reason why hard money is so much faster, and one of the biggest reasons is the loan approval process for hard money is much faster. A community bank's lending committee might meet once a week and go over all of the loans that they are looking to approve in the near future. This discussion and approval process slows the lending process down tremendously. In hard money lending, there's an urgency in time management and decision-making. As a result, there is a hierarchy of time between your borrowing choices. The fact that you can get loan approval while you are on the phone with your hard money lender is not a small thing.

Generally, hard money can close in a week or less, normal community banks, maybe two weeks if you have an established credit line, but usually the community bank takes up to three weeks to close. Normal thirty-year mortgages take about a month to close. Of course, cash is king—you can close immediately with cash. That's the hierarchy of timing, from the top to the bottom: cash, hard money, soft money, and normal mortgage.

A lot of times, timing is where it's at, because it is being driven by the seller. They want to sell their house quickly! In those cases, cash and hard money are king. For example, there is a house for sale for $300,000. If someone offers at the asking price but they are thirty days out from closing a loan and someone else comes along, who is using hard money, and they offer a seller who is looking for a quick sale at $20,000 less than the asking price, nine times out of ten the seller will take the faster, hard money offer over the higher one.

When we lend out our money, it is essentially a short-term rental of funds that lasts anywhere between three and six months. For us, the less time the borrower uses our money, the better our economic return. The points we earn increase our return so the more times we can loan the same money out, the higher our returns. For example, if we are doing a $100,000 loan, with one point on the loan at $1,000, this means that if we give out this $100,000 loan at 12 percent interest with a three-point origination fee, we are getting $3,000 up front when the loan closes. Keep in mind the payment is $1,000 a month. So, if I go out at 12 percent and three points and it's a one-year loan, that's a 15 percent return on that money. If I go out at 12 percent and three points, for that same $100,000, and they pay us back in three months and we do two more loans that same year with the same $100,000 the effective yield is 24 percent because we are getting our normal 12 percent interest for the money but we are getting three points from four different originations. Our general goal is to get an 18 percent annual return, which means we are trying to do 12 percent and three points for six months on the average loan.

We once had a borrower who lived in Leesburg, Virginia, and he had found two decent properties that were in Baltimore, Maryland. This doesn't inherently seem like a bad thing. But if you know anything about these areas, you'd know that, on a good day with no traffic, Leesburg to Baltimore takes about ninety minutes, but with traffic, it can take up to three hours. We provided 100 percent financing for this deal. The borrower had a long commute to the properties and no money of his own in the game. The commute was so much trouble he just gave up on his projects and we took them back as REOs. Ultimately, he was too far away to look after the renovations properly. So now, whenever we are evaluating a borrower's loan, we find out how close the borrower lives to the asset that they are improving. If the proximity is too far away, we will turn them down immediately.

Traditional Mortgages

Again, it's time to reference your earlier bookmark and reread the financial literacy section on mortgages. I will not go back over what traditional mortgages are in detail, but they are very useful instruments in building a rental portfolio. Yes, more documentation is needed to get a traditional mortgage than for less conventional financing, but getting one provides you with the longest amortization schedule and the lowest interest rate loan product which improves the cash flow on your rental property.

One of the strategies that I have used over the years is to purchase my primary residence with a low-interest-rate, thirty-year-fixed mortgage, obtain a home equity line of credit (later in this chapter), buy another house, and turn the owner-occupied house into a rental. The problem with this strategy is that you can only have a defined number of mortgages or HELOCs (home equity lines of credit) in your name. The number used to be ten. As a matter of fact, I could not even get a traditional mortgage today because I have maxed out the number of personal loans for which I can qualify! Attaching the HELOC to your primary home is smart because it adds to your liquidity. You can then use what we call "dead equity" for future investments. You don't want to tie up your equity in losing investments or spend it down, so be careful! The biggest issue with traditional mortgages is the amount of documentation required and the time it takes to get them established. Of all financing options, these mortgages take the longest time to get.

The good news about VA and FHA mortgages is that they are assumable. In times of higher interest rates, assuming a VA or FHA loan is a good idea. Loan assumptions transfer the existing loan balance, interest rate, and payments to the new purchaser. You do not have to have the military service requirement to assume a VA loan. In both cases, the lender has to approve your income and credit history. VA assumption requires you to pay a 0.5 percent funding fee of the loan balance. So, if you have an assumable loan at a low rate and a great house to sell, you have two assets on the market at one time!

Owner Financing

The name is somewhat self-explanatory, but owner financing is a crucial tool when doing creative financing. Owner financing, often called seller financing, occurs when the seller finances the buyer's purchase using the seller's equity in their house. It is an alternative to a mortgage. Seller financing can be done quicker and cheaper than a normal mortgage. Aspects of owner-financed deals are negotiable from the interest rate to the down payment to the length of loan and amortization schedule. Usually, the owner owns the property outright, but in cases where the owner does not own the property outright, they can offer a second mortgage behind the first mortgage. The purchaser can either do a subject-to (next section) the first mortgage or assume the first mortgage provided it is a VA or FHA loan described earlier.

Seller financing provides many potential advantages to both buyers and sellers, such as the terms are negotiable, application documentation is not required, and the deal can close in a week or less. The seller can also use this as an installment contract and avoid paying hefty capital gains at once and wield it as a nice annuity source of income. Unfortunately, the biggest problem with seller financing is that these deals are hard to find! Once you are on the owner's side, however, this is a method you might consider to sell your property for a stable, relatively passive return as we discuss at the end of the book.

Subject to the Existing Mortgage (Subject-To Deals)

Another creative way to finance deals is by taking ownership of the property *subject to* the existing mortgage. A purchaser/investor takes the rights to the title for a property while the seller's existing mortgage stays in place, hence, "subject to " the current mortgage. Note: this is not the same as assuming the loan. There is no formal bank approval process. The bank does not even know that this is going on unless they are notified by the purchaser or current note holder. The purchaser/investor simply takes over payments on an existing loan. The purchaser incurs no liability to repay the loan.

However, most mortgages have a "due on sale" clause, so the lender has the right, not the obligation, to call the note due in full when this happens. If the new purchaser keeps the loan/hazardous insurance current it is very unlikely that the lender will call the note. We have never heard of an instance where a lender has called a note due in full without an insurance or default issue. Why is that you might ask? Banks would rather keep a performing loan going before they spend time and money originating a new loan with unknown risks of default.

Subject-to financing is a great vehicle for investors wanting to fix/flip and/or buy and hold. The biggest advantage is the interest rate and the terms of the existing note. If they are better than the current market, you have a bonus on your cash flow. Why else would you do a subject-to if you could not take advantage of the interest rate? One good reason would be that you can't qualify for the loan without doing a subject-to-transaction. When you take over someone else's loan, your payments on the loan are further into the amortization schedule, meaning you have less time left to pay off the loan than the original term of the loan. One more disadvantage exists for this type of loan: the former owner is still on the hook for the obligation. This should never be a problem if you are buying the property in a sizable equity position as you need to do. The seller is protected by the buyer's risk of losing their down payment if they default.

Debt Service Coverage Ratio Loans (DSCR)

A debt service coverage ratio is a commercial real estate loan for buy-and-hold investors. The rental income of the property is the key qualifier. Is the property generating enough income to pay the mortgage? This type of loan can be done on a single property or a portfolio of properties. We have done DSCR loans many times in our careers. DSCR loans can be flexible depending on the lender. Sometimes you can even pick your amortization schedule. The larger the DSCR ratio is, the more income there is to pay the loan. DSCR is calculated below.

Property Rents / PITI(A) = DSCR

PITIA = Principal, Interest, Taxes, Insurance and Home Association (Condo) Dues

$2,500 Rents / $2,000 Payment = 1.25 DSCR

The higher the DSCR, the lower the interest rate the bank is willing to provide. Generally, the bank is not looking for a personal income requirement with a DSCR loan.

Home Equity Lines of Credit (HELOCs)

The biggest advantage of homeownership is the ability to build equity over time. Home equity is created in one of three ways: market appreciation, paying the principal down over time, or paying the loan amount down as a lump sum payment. You can use the equity in your home to secure low-cost funds in the form of a HELOC. A HELOC is basically a checkbook tied to the equity of your house. It is a great tool for increasing your liquidity (I know, I used that word again). The way it works is that banks will take the appraised value of your home and multiply it by a factor. Most banks use 75 percent, but in better economic times I have seen this increase to 90 percent on owner-occupied homes, and subtract out the balance left on the first mortgage. The result is the highest amount of credit the bank can offer on your property.

For example, let's assume that you have lived in your primary residence for ten years. The market has been exceptionally good and your home's appraised value is now $600,000. Your first mortgage payoff is $250,000. If banks are giving a 75 percent HELOC, you can establish a HELOC to tap into the $350,000 of equity. That is $600,000 x 0.75 ($450,000) minus $250,000. That makes your HELOC limit $200,000. You can use this $200,000 to purchase an investment property. The amount you can borrow is typically capped by the lender at some percentage of the LTV; in our example, we used 75 percent.

This is an incredible tool for you to take advantage of during your real estate investing career. This is definitely good for investors in levels one through three. If you do not remember what this is, go back to your bookmarks in chapter two.

Do you remember the earlier story about my home purchase using credit cards? Well guess what: I bought my next house to live in at the courthouse steps and it was vacant! The house was located right in the neighborhood where I wanted to live. When the house came up for auction, I went to the courthouse steps to bid. It was a first trust foreclosure and I knew there was a second trust. It was 2008 and we were right in the middle of the foreclosure crisis. The second trust did not even show up to bid on their interest. I was the only bidder that day on the house and got the house for $625,000. At the time, the market value was around $800,000. There was just one problem. I did not have $625,000 in cash.

On the positive side, I did have great credit, income, and some cash. During the foreclosure crisis, we were REO agents. We were selling hundreds of homes on behalf of the banks at that time. One of the services we did for the banks was to re-key the houses if they were vacant. So, on this particular house, I needed a conventional loan with a 20 percent down payment ($125,000), leaving me with a mortgage of $500,000, but, more importantly, an equity position of $300,000. The problem was since I was getting a conventional mortgage, they needed an appraiser to access the house. Before I owned the house I had it rekeyed and turned on the utilities so I could get an appraisal. Voila! I closed on the purchase with a traditional mortgage.

Now, fast forward the story about a year. There was a nice manager at M&T Bank where I had my business account. I was going by the bank two or three times a week to deposit crazy commission checks with a few fix-and-flip profit checks sprinkled in. It was a great time for my income because we were selling so many bank houses at the time. The M&T manager began asking me questions. I am sure he was also monitoring my account balances and was making an effort to get me to do more business with the bank. One day I said to him, "Fine, let me try and get a HELOC on my house." Keep in mind, at this point, I owned eight rentals with Sam (loans in our personal names at the time), had a mortgage with an ex-wife, and also had a mortgage and HELOC on the credit card house. I knew I was not getting a HELOC from M&T. About a week later I was depositing even more commission checks, a quarterly check from owning a title company, when Mr. M&T asked me to come into his office. He looked really sad. He told me the bad news, even though my credit score was in the high 780s, and I had enough equity in my primary residence, he could not get me the HELOC because I had too many mortgages in my name! I started smiling and laughing and told him not to worry about it because it wasn't his fault. He was relieved, but discouraged, that he could not get me that HELOC! He really wanted to help me.

Believe it or not, once you find the deal, the money is not that far behind. In our opinion, finding the deals is where the money is. Keep in mind that you make the money on the buy side by entering the right deal. In other words, you can quickly lose money if you pay too much for property. However, real estate can be forgiving if you make a bad purchase and simply hold the asset as a rental. An appreciating market might bail you out sometime in the future.

I bet you thought finding the money would be hard! In fact, it is not so hard to find money once you have a deal. You need to do your financing planning and preparation before you find your deal though. That way you know how your execution will play out. Each deal that you find with enough equity can, and, will be financed. The only question is how you will fund the deal. It is better to have done some planning around your financing before you get your deal so you aren't under pressure at the time of closing.

Key Takeaways

- Know your potential sources of financing.
- Know which form of available financing will help you get your best deal.
- Select financing that best fits your investment needs.
- Always be well prepared to finance deals you find.

Chapter 11

FIXING, FLIPPING, AND OTHER WAYS TO PROFIT FROM DISTRESS

"Profitability is the sovereign criterion of the enterprise."
—Peter Drucker

In February 2019, we bought a foreclosure home in DC. Now, something you need to know before investing in DC is that renters have rights that transfer with ownership. So hypothetically, you could buy a house with a renter that has a ten-year lease, and this will stand as a valid contract, even though you weren't party to it when it was created. And just like that, you have a problem, a decade of potential problems. We learned this the hard way. Not long after purchasing the property, we found it came with a tenant who had a lease in hand. We had stepped into a battle as the tenant had hired a lawyer who specialized in keeping people with questionable rights in homes or demanding money in exchange for them leaving. We needed to think about our profit margin, and we couldn't afford this problem to drag on for years.

So, we made the tenant an offer of $10,000 to leave. This was swiftly met with a counteroffer— $200,000 for their cooperation. This was twenty times our original offer, and it wasn't the kind of bargaining we had in mind. For tenants, it's often a win-win. Either they convince the buyers to accept their counter-offer or they continue living in a property at below-market rent. If the tenant presents a below-market rent (even rent for a dollar a month) the new landlord in DC can be required to honor that lease. So, you must inspect properties yourself before you sign on the dotted line. Don't send someone to do it on your behalf! If you slip up and end up buying a property containing tenants on a long-term (below market) lease, you could find your renovation plans dragging on for months or years longer than you budgeted for or anticipated.

This is why it is so important to have access to a good real estate attorney. Remember Ed? He brings a lot to the team and he knows how to deal with situations like this very well. Ed isn't just great at contractual stuff; he is also an ace at prepping the final stages of selling a home, with his eyes firmly wired to the end game. Ed did an unbelievable job when it came to dealing with the lease this family had given us. Instead of just accepting the document at face value, he prepared to go all the way, right down to examining the forensics of the signatures. While carefully dissecting the seemingly valid lease, he spotted a faint watermark from a website–a website where you could download lease templates and make a proper lease or fake up a fraudulent lease!

Bingo! We had them. As a result of this enlightening discovery, Ed subpoenaed the internet company based in Canada and they sent him a comprehensive log, detailing keystroke to keystroke how this fraudulent document was created, complete with a date and time stamp. After proving the document was a fake created after our foreclosure, we paid the initial fee that we'd offered the tenants—$10k and they were gone. This was a fortunate escape because we had a lawyer like Ed who would not just throw up his hands when given a superficially valid contract. We have been far more careful to avoid unwanted guests and holdover tenants ever since, including bedbugs, but I have already told you that story.

Why would we still pay the tenants who presented a fake lease? In DC, working through the courts (even when you win) is such a lengthy process that it is easier to come to terms with a tenant who has an expired lease, or fake lease in this case, and get them to take some money to move out quickly. Unfortunately, it takes so long to evict someone in DC, that paying them to leave is cheaper even than waiting for the sheriff to come to enforce a valid eviction.

Note Purchases

If a bank loans someone money through a mortgage to buy a house and they become unable to make repayments, the note on the house will be eligible for a foreclosure sale. However, sometimes homeowners are hard to deal with, such as those with mental health issues or combative types who will fight tooth and nail to stay put, and the banks don't want to deal with that kind of social problem (they don't want to dirty their three-piece suits). It's just not the kind of publicity they want. So, another option for the banks is selling the debt, in the form of a real estate note. The note is an agreement between a borrower and lender where the borrower agrees to repay the lender under the terms laid out in the note. Often these notes are sold to other banks but sometimes they come to investors like us.

Let's say we have purchased a distressed asset via a real estate note. In this case, we can either foreclose or get a deed instead of foreclosure from the borrower. Then we can fix up the place with whatever it needs, sell it, and make a profit. Alternatively, we can continue to pass the note along and sell it to someone else in a similar position who might find value in the property. If they value it more than we do, we can sell the note at a profit. Often, when we have dealt with notes, we have bought into extremely wacky and weird situations. Overall, there are legal issues that the banks want to avoid. As the note passes between owners before it is "cured," this process is called "distressed carries." In most scenarios, the banks are usually selling distressed notes which are in their second or third position.

The second position means that you had the first trust with the likes of Citibank or Bank of America, let's say for $300,000. The house could be worth $600,000, but somebody has a second trust for $100,000 on top of the $300,000. A defaulted note that is in the second or third position tends to be picked up by smaller institutions, or loan brokers, who often like to get their hands on these. We know a couple of contacts throughout the country that work with distressed carriers, but as regional players, we're only interested in anything in DC, Maryland, or Virginia. As a rule, we don't buy second trusts in areas that we don't know well. This means our exposure to this kind of work is limited, but we do get our hands on a few notes.

Here is an example of our experience involving an unwanted secondary note that was sold to us by a bank. We paid a visit to a woman living in a pre-foreclosure home. Chatting to her downstairs she seemed pretty normal, but after checking out the floor above, we realized we had stumbled on another, shall we say, quirky individual. When we entered the room upstairs, we were surprised to find it decked out with aluminum cans and tin-foil accessories. She then explained that she was communicating with the mothership and this is how she did it. We had unintentionally stumbled upon Barbarella's HQ (shout out to Jane Fonda). Meanwhile, her husband was doing time in jail for reasons we didn't know. Despite thinking she was from another planet, she was well enough to sign the deed and her husband was able to do a jailhouse closing. As weird as this all was, you have to listen to people when they are telling you about their lives, no matter how whacky or insane they might seem. No doubt the previous owners of the note didn't have time for her and we wanted to end the cycle of contempt. Respect costs nothing but is very good for business. If you don't try to engage with homeowners, you'll find it much harder to manage the distressed asset.

And now for another tale that comes with a warning. In 2015, we bought a house from an auction that had failed to sell at five prior auctions. It was a townhouse that had two parking spaces in front of it that were always empty. As a result, we had assumed the property was vacant (yep, you know where this is going). Unbeknownst to me, when you don't pay your homeowner association (HOA) dues, they take your assigned parking privileges away or they'll tow your vehicle. iTherefore, the occupant had been parking his vehicle on the other side of the road. Anyway, after buying the property on the courthouse steps I stopped by the house and delivered an occupancy note, which said something along the lines of: "Hey, this is Charlie, we just bought this property, here are your options..." The occupant was a 70-year-old military vet, who had worked as an engineer and had earned a decent living. Naturally, we were slightly confused as to why he was struggling to pay his mortgage every month. He was living off of social security checks and was foreclosed on a very small loan amount— he was only $1,000 behind on the loan. After meeting with him, we realized that he's probably suffering from one of the big three: drugs, alcohol, or gambling. He was so skinny I immediately assumed drugs were his undoing.

I spent a good eight hours with this friendly vet, talking with him about his life, career, and family before checking out the entire house. Just as I was leaving, he stopped me, "One second, I have to grab something out of my car." So, I walked with him towards his car, which to my surprise was a BMW. This wasn't the car you'd expect from someone whose property was foreclosed, a relic of his more successful days no doubt. As he rummaged in the front, I peered through the back window(what can I say, I can be nosey)–the whole backseat was loaded with merchandise from Caesars and MGM.

Gambling! He must have gambled away his pension fund. We chatted some more and it was clear that this was indeed the problem. He had gambled away his 401k and after losing it all he was hooked on playing the daily lottery. I asked him if he would be willing to live in a senior independent living facility. Thankfully, he agreed and moved into one that I located about a mile away. Before foreclosure, he was short on his payments by 200 bucks a month. The trouble was he was taking his Social Security checks and going straight to the casino. His skinny physique wasn't caused by drugs at all, he was just broke and so obsessed with gambling that he spent his money at the casino instead of feeding himself properly.

A few days before he was set to move out of the townhouse, one of our handymen, we call him "The W," because he is our superhero, went to the house to help the vet with his move. When The W peered in through the window, he saw the vet lying still on his bed facing up at the ceiling. The W kept knocking and yelling his name but the vet didn't move. The W called me and I drove over right away.

"Is he playing possum?" The W asked.

"Are you kidding me? He might be dead, call 9-1-1!"

Fortunately, once the ambulance got there, they were able to resuscitate him. Apparently, he had an OD on insulin. After that night, he got some help at the hospital for a week and ended up moving to a senior living facility where he lived for five years. We were subsidizing his rent that entire time and he was able to see the birth of a grandkid. He eventually gave up gambling, led a relatively normal life, and was able to revive his family relationships. So, from losing it all and having a near-death experience, our vet transformed his life into one of positivity.

Unfortunately, not all our stories end so well. We had another tenant/occupant I'll call Tom; the owners of the house had asked us to buy this rental back in 2016. They wanted us to buy the home because they didn't want to evict Tom–yep you read that right, it seemed a bit weird to us too. After visiting, we found out that earlier in his life, Tom was forced to live in this crawl space of the house– he had suffered under the regime of an extremely abusive mother, who had died a few years prior. The whole situation was horrendous. Tom had worked at the supermarket at the seafood counter for many years but he had recently lost his job after losing his driver's license because of a DUI.

When we arrived, the entire front yard was full of beer cans and bottles, and every square inch of the half-acre yard was covered. We got along with Tom and he seemed to like us. We knew people he knew and vice versa. He played the guitar and was a bright guy, which only made his unfortunate situation seem sadder. After a few meetings with us, he agreed to move out into a basement rental across town. Then tragedy struck a few days before his move-in date. Tom took his own life. He was mentally traumatized and psychologically trapped in the house; instead of leaving it, he chose to kill himself inside it. Plenty of our dealings are relatively normal, but when you are trading in distressed assets, you will come across some unusual and often sad situations. So, be prepared.

Practicing empathy, listening, and finding solutions to people's problems are skills you need to master when managing a pre-foreclosure. You need to offer this kind of human support and respect from day one. When you are trying to get someone to leave their home because they cannot afford or deal with it, kindness needs to be at the heart of everything you do. Simply throwing money at socially neglected people is never the solution. Those who have fallen on the hardest of times need a foundation to work from, they need to build back a framework to escape the cycle of misfortune or abuse that has befallen them.

A great example of this is our 70-year-old veteran gambler. If we had given him a lump of money right when we met him, he would have spent that faster than you could blink. Instead, we were able to help him regain the framework of his life and reconnect him to his family and friends so he could function as a valued member of society. This side of the job is hard but also immensely rewarding. We are not social workers. We are real estate investors, but we are human beings first and foremost. So, be kind when you are in the business of buying people's homes.

A key takeaway from this chapter is simple but important—doing well by doing good. Some of our competitors just file foreclosure or eviction on a property, they won't even talk to the people living in the house. They'll throw the full might of the legal system at these people, beating them with it until they're out. In reality, it costs less time and money to exercise some empathy and connect with these people rather than paying lawyers to do your dirty work. And we sleep well at night.

Fixing and Flipping

Generally, when people think of fixing and flipping, they might think of taking an old beater, investing a ton of money into it, and then selling it for much more than they paid for it. Well, parts of that can be true. You can indeed invest in a beater and pour huge amounts of money into it with the hope of selling it for a profit, but that's risky, very risky, especially if you don't have a lot of capital. For those of you not keen on playing Russian roulette with your savings, we have developed four tiers within the fixing and flipping umbrella. Those four tiers are as follows:

The First Tier

This is the simplest and quickest option (sounds tempting, doesn't it?). You buy the property and make repairs to the house to make it functional. You do not do any cosmetic repairs. This is called the wholetail (wholesale + retail) model. You buy the house off-market at a wholesale price and sell it on the Multiple Listing Service (MLS) at a retail price slightly lower than other comparable properties to get a quick sale. We have done this many times with our courthouse buys. If we deem the property vacant and in good shape, we simply purchase the property at the courthouse steps, close on it in two weeks or less, re-key it, and then put it back on the MLS.

The Second Tier

This is the next best option from a time and risk management perspective. You buy the property, clean it out, give it a fresh lick of paint, lay some new carpets, or wax the floorboards, and call it a day. You can list this kind of property far quicker than those falling under the third and fourth tiers. These are great projects to find because the overhead costs are low. Essentially, the more fixing up necessary, the more cost control issues you are likely to encounter. So, treat these second-tier opportunities as a blessing.

The anticipated costs should prove to be largely accurate unless you are unlucky enough to find some skeletons in the closet that were undisclosed. If you find a skeleton or two, this could push the property into a completely new tier of its own! However, a prudent and comprehensive review of the property before you purchase it should prevent your quick-fix-up dream from becoming a nightmare. Even with the best inspections and planning you can run into problems. Our contractor *literally* found a skeleton in the closet of a house we were renovating. That, however, is a whole different story. So that's tier two, the starting point of fix and flip, which we call "dressing the pig."

The Third Tier

This is where things start to get a little more expensive (I can hear your wallets groaning already). We're talking new bathroom(s), complete kitchen refits, brand new flooring, painting, and drywalling— the list can go on. Obviously, with higher overhead expenses and a longer fixing period, there is more risk with tier three. However, for those with the appetite, with higher risk comes the opportunity for greater reward (usually).

These projects present a potentially profitable opportunity to transform the asset. By transformation, we mean that an unwelcoming house can be turned into one that is attractive to a buyer in the market. Perhaps a patchwork of projects and repairs coupled with some dated features make a house undesirable. If you get into that house and create continuity of design by opening the floor plan, putting a consistent floor type in, and installing a walk-in shower without doors, you will attract a different kind of consumer. If the house is downtown, where there are lots of small bedrooms, you can renovate it to have a master suite bathroom with fewer rooms, thus making your house more appealing to a different market segment. That sort of transformation can unlock market value.

This is a riskier and more complicated renovation that requires finesse to make the right choices, but it can really boost the value of the flip. By "the right choice," I mean you have to get the property at a lower price to account for the potential costs and/or have a transformation plan that will substantially increase the value of the property much more than the repair cost.

The Fourth Tier

Now, finally, we get to the big boy—the fourth tier. This is where we start to get into changes that require new plans and permits. This is your plumbing, major electrical work, HVAC, and total reconfiguration, and in some cases, this can only be scratching the surface of what fixing needs to be done. You might have to add a two-car garage, deliver power to the garage, add a bedroom over the garage, convert attic space to living space, convert a three-season room to fully integrated living space, connect the property to the public sewer, or completely rework a failed septic field. You might have to gut the house down to the studs and build an entirely new interior.

It's usually in your best interest to try and avoid homes like this, particularly when you are just getting started. But for those who can stomach high risk, have the commitment, and have a good handle on assessing repair needs and costs, these properties can give you the best returns. Heck, we made $100,000 on a house that was nothing more than a brick shell with no roof and no floors (I mean no floor joists, not no hardwoods). How? We paid $30,000 cash for the property. The brick was gorgeous and in perfect shape so we used a construction loan to spend $250,000 on putting in floors and a roof—literally, everything but the walls. The effectively brand-new house sold for $475,000. Remember cash on cash return? How does 300 percent in less than six months sound?

The real kicker to watch out for in this category is permitting. Here's my philosophy on that: get freaking lost. As a general rule, you want property where you need no special permits. This should not be much of a problem if you are replacing what is there with like kind, e.g., gutting an old kitchen and replacing it with a new kitchen in the same spot with the same plumbing and electrical locations.

Avoid as much permitting beyond this as possible as the process will drain your time and leach your energy and patience. You'll find yourself dealing with third-party permitting inspectors that don't have the same fire under their butts to get this place fixed up as you do, and thus increase your carrying costs. In this respect, you lose a degree of control over the project and the unaccounted cost can spiral. If that doesn't put you off, it's worth knowing that every jurisdiction has different regulations governing how much work can be done before the county inspector needs to review the work in progress. They'll be looking for health and safety issues, fire hazards, structural concerns, and such. It's kind of like the Grim Reaper turning up at your door and you're hoping he isn't there to kill off your project.

Even more dangerous is buying a property that you value based on your expectations that you can expand or substantially change the existing footprint and overall layout. That two-bedroom might double or triple in value if you just close in the carport walls to make it have two more bedrooms. But can you really do that given local building codes? Don't assume you can just add a garage or addition on top of an existing driveway as any number of setbacks and other requirements could block you. In other words, don't assume you can get a permit for whatever you dream up, no matter how much it *should* make sense to the jurisdiction!

We knew we'd have to pull permits with the shell example discussed before, but we were using the same footprint inside the existing brick walls, meaning we could rebuild by right without any special exception in that jurisdiction. Still one of our biggest delays (we are talking months here) was getting the power company to come out to put in a new electrical connection and meter because the shell had sat without any for so many years.

My advice here won't come as a surprise. When it comes to fourth-tier properties, I highly recommend avoiding them unless you are *very* experienced. It's best to steer clear of properties that call for additions, excavations, septic systems, extensions, or that have foundation issues and the like. Inexperienced investors will quickly find themselves out of their depths and struggling to keep the project on time and within budget. So, unless you can afford to fail, just don't bother. Wait instead until you have a few million in your bank from your tier one, two, and three investments, and then take yourself to your doctor for a full-service checkup–you'll need a healthy heart to endure that road ahead.

Never forget that simple inexperience can be expensive. When new investors find a property that requires major changes, they often turn to a third-party contractor to deliver them. This is extremely risky, even if you have a good contractor. You won't know their day-to-day schedule so you cannot guarantee the reliable timetable that such a project requires. More importantly, they may uncover major faults within the property, which of course they are not responsible for, and this can end up costing you a lot of money. Also, don't forget your time is valuable. If one big, profitable project takes all of your time to manage for six months when instead you could find and complete two easier projects in ninety days, there is a good chance you'll make a lot more money keeping things simple. Either way, make sure you factor this consideration into your planning and approach.

What Should You Fix to Flip?

Enough putting you off, let's talk about the opportunities you should embrace. So, you've just bought yourself your first investment property —a house that falls in tier two, most likely. You are going to ask yourself;

"Where do I start?"' Great question! You need to be thinking strategically. Just throwing pails of paint around without a plan in place will leave you with a bigger mess and more repair costs than when you started. Start spending your repair budget on what you see first because this is what the buyer will see first.

The landscape in the front of the house is the first thing you see, so, you guessed it, it is the first thing that you should be investing in. You are also giving trees, shrubs, and flowerbeds, whatever the case may be, a chance to grow and flourish so that by the time the rest of the house is done, it should look mighty spiffy. Next, the door handle to the property is important. I know that may seem like a funny second choice, but seriously, it's the first thing they'll touch. If they feel a hollow, slightly wobbly, bargain store knob in their hand, then subconsciously, they'll look at the rest of the property as cheap and unsubstantial. Little details like this won't break the bank but will create the right impression, so don't be cheap or it may cost you in the long run. Take a look at the driveway. Does the asphalt need a fresh coat of sealer to make it look new? If it is concrete, it might need to be power washed. Cracks in asphalt or concrete *must* be filled. A ratty-looking driveway will raise questions about the maintenance of the unseen parts of the property.

After you have worked on creating the right first impression, next comes the staging of the home. There are little hacks realtors use to block out aspects of the property that could be undesirable to a potential buyer. I am not talking about putting a tall lampshade in front of a bad case of rising dampness that shows on the wall, or spraying a ton of air freshener to cover the smell of the decomposing body hidden under the floorboards. Those issues, by the way, you need to fix. We did purchase a house with a decomposing body in the floorboards once. That requires a different approach and that story is for another day, but we fixed it completely! However, some things aren't fixable, like street noise, for example. Some savvy realtors will attempt to block out or neutralize street noise by playing ambient music throughout the property or perhaps have a fireplace scene playing on a mounted TV, with the crackling turned up nice and high.

As you get into fixing and selling more eclectic homes that are less cookie-cutter, you will want to have a unique, eye-catching feature on each floor. Do this even if it's a bit polarizing to consumer tastes. An example of such a feature might be a special treatment to a skylight, like installing wood around it. Or it could be a nice contemporary light fixture or a piece of stained glass installed in a transom—something unique that will catch the buyer's eye. A buyer will know they can remove the modern art piece from the staging that they don't like. What they need to see is a feature that they do like that is permanent. In city houses, exposed brick walls that gleam with a glossy sealant finish or a small green space outside will do the trick. Don't go too far off the mainstream in color selections; look at big brand paint advertising and see what neutrals they are promoting this year. That can be a great choice to create a modern space in which any buyer can picture themselves.

You're best to avoid artwork that conveys sex, politics, or religion, though, as these issues are more personal than simply a question of taste (so graphic prints of scantily dressed nuns with AK-47s would better be replaced by a simple abstract print from your nearest Ikea). Anyway, there are many ways to give each part of the home a unique touch that solidifies the property in the buyer's mind. That's the goal.

If you are in the market for ease and speed, then look no further than a vanilla whole-tail house (tier one). It is a plain vanilla home that is eligible for FHA financing. FHA financing requires an appraisal or inspection to make sure things function correctly and that there's no chipping paint and things of that nature; nothing much to worry about. Once the home is inspected and deemed to be livable, you then bring it up to whole tail. Yes, you read that correctly. This is not a fishing term, but rather the position in between wholesale and retail. This means the property could be bought and lived in or a further investment could be made to take it to the next level. If it's the latter, the money, time, and effort invested need to generate a return relative to that investment. However, a lot of people who are starting in this business will start by buying plain vanilla homes and reselling them. Projects like this are great for building experience and confidence in the industry. Even though the returns are not as handsome, this is a sensible place to start.

When you are spearheading a renovation project as a newbie, it is essential that you get on top of contractor management. You need to get different quotes from various general contractors (GCs) in your area. Once you've received quotes from various local GCs, you need to decide whether you want to approach the best GC candidate and give them the project or if you want to directly employ subcontractors yourself. There are a couple of big benefits from employing subcontractors directly.

First, a good general contractor gets paid approximately 10 to 20 percent of the job's total cost. You can save this money if you do it yourself. However, there is a lot of work they are doing and expertise they are using to get the 10 to 20 percent fee income. Keep in mind that general contractors coordinate jobs, look for discounted products to use, and make sure that every design choice is made with the overall project in mind.

The second big benefit is that you are closely involved with the project and can make decisions on the fly that fit your overall view of how the project should turn out. But be forewarned: you might not like your own choices, and if there are any problems at all between trades such as plumbers, electricians, and carpenters, those problems will be yours to resolve.

Whichever route you decide, you cannot just sit back and do nothing. There will still be various project management tasks you need to complete, such as picking out the finishes, determining any changes to the space (like moving walls), picking out appliances, and deciding on the quality/price of HVAC as well as mechanical equipment. No matter which route you choose, you have to be involved. To ensure your project runs smoothly, you need to retain a degree of responsibility, regardless of how much you trust your contractors.

Checking in at least once a week will prevent issues from developing and problems growing in severity without your knowledge. Even the best contractors and workers will be aware that you come frequently to look around or never show up at all. Which do you think is better for them to expect?

With bigger projects, we'd recommend that you check in with your GC every day, once a week is the bare minimum.

In 2003, we were beginning our careers and were newbies who hadn't got to grips with the tricks of the trade. We came across a house on a street where we already owned four properties–like a real-life game of Monopoly. One of these was a rental and the other three were flips. This new offering seemed like another fix-flip-and-move-on opportunity.

Upon inspecting the property, we realized the house needed a lot of attention. It was a foundation block house and the entire building was tilting to one side as it was sinking into the foundations. This was the result of years of neglect, with pipe leaks causing extreme water damage. Three-quarters of the house was submerged underground. The living room was now a basement! This was quite an undertaking for a team of newbies, bearing in mind that most of our wider contractor connections were also relatively new to the industry. How many inexperienced investors does it take to change a light bulb? The reality was, that we couldn't, this was beyond our experience level and, like the sinking property, we were in too deep. Trouble is, we had already bought the house. Oops. Maurice, our GC, was very new to the game, too. When we took him through the house for the first time, his jaw dropped to the floor like something out of Looney Tunes.

The house was so badly submerged in the ground that Maurice had to come in with a hydraulic press lifter and raise the whole property so he could replace the old beams and rebuild the interior. This allowed him to unblock the foundations and then reblock them. After lifting the property, he then sealed it from the inside out. As you may have guessed, we didn't make much profit on this property, but what we gained was a hell of a learning experience.

In 2007, we bought an REO (real estate-owned) house from an auction website. All of the houses on these auction websites were bank-owned, so the only way to know if the house was vacant was by looking at the pictures available. That was the extent of the access we had—photos on a webpage. We were doing such a high volume of work at the time that we sometimes just skimmed over the photos and the other information listed. We focused on the "main stuff," like how many bedrooms and bathrooms there were and we were somewhat blasé about the details. We found a vacant house that was listed as a four-bed and one-bath property. We were not able to walk through the house and inspect it before we made our bid. Being the high-volume players that we were, we were just bidding on houses left, right, and center, without ever seeing them in person. "Fuck that!" we thought. "What a waste of time." We were going to the courthouse steps and buying the houses. We had referrals from realtors and deals from wholesalers, so business was certainly moving. Actually, it was absolute madness!

This particular house that we had bought on a whim was a single-family with four bedrooms and two and a half baths. Upon visiting the house, we were shocked to find a bedroom missing. The bank had miscounted the bedrooms (there were only three!) and had priced the house based on this misrepresentation. This changed the value of the house considerably. Fortunately, this wasn't a make-or-break deal for us because we had so much capital that we had budgeted for setbacks like this. Had we been a far more modest operation, with just a house or two at any given time, a slip like this could have easily put us out of business.

I mentioned staging earlier in the chapter, but it deserves a second mention as it can be a make or break for the property as trends change and things ebb and flow in and out of style. For example, we had a house that we staged in a contemporary style that wasn't the most popular for a conventional neighborhood. We realized this, took the house off the market, restaged it with contemporary Colonial American furnishings, and placed it back on the market. With a new style in place, it sold within two weeks of re-listing. At times, you can stage a house in a way that is unique and like nothing else on the market, but there's a limit. It's important not to stray too far from conventional tastes. You want it to be just different enough to make viewers do a double take and look more closely but not so different that they can't envision themselves in it.

Another thing a newbie needs to properly understand is the process of finding a realtor. Expect to be doing three interviews a day until you find someone who will be able to sell a pen better than Brad Bodnick (and that is a *Wolf of Wall Street* film reference, for those of you not in the know). Don't worry if they're unpleasant or difficult; if they can sell houses, keep them around. This obviously doesn't go for all of your employees and associates; you need trustworthy and accountable people for the administrative work. To be honest, you probably won't find a great real estate agent for a while. After over 1,000 sales and tons of agents, we have probably only had five really decent ones. Some just phone it in, figuring the house will sell at some point and 3 percent of $400,000 with zero effort is tempting over 3 percent of $450,000 with hours of thought, marketing, open houses, etc. Meanwhile, that $50,000 is probably all profit for you, and might be all of your profit. In other words, selling a house at its most profitable number is a ton of work for a realtor. They must be totally dedicated and focused if they are going to be very successful while also making you money. This is a rare find but persevere in your search because these agents do exist.

Pitfalls with Fix and Flips

When you're starting out, you need to keep a firm eye on your renovation expenses. Often, they go over budget because of unexpected finds in the house, such as plumbing or electrical issues, termite damage, or other hidden problems. Not budgeting for this kind of thing is often detrimental to rehab companies. Another pitfall is to put a home up for sale when it may be better suited and thus valued as a rental property. Toward the end of the foreclosure crisis in 2009, Ed picked up a great property at auction he planned to flip but thought also could be a good rental. Prices were stagnating or worse when it was ready for sale, so he didn't get the buyer interest or number he wanted. He stuck the property in our rental portfolio where it still sits today (at a much higher asset valuation). In other words, it is so important to consider multiple options in your exit strategy *before* buying and to know the potential worth and alternative disposition of the property you want to purchase.

Renting can be great, but it is a commitment of time on your part. If you are not set up to do it, it can be too much. If you are not ready to provide your potential tenants with a great living experience, including being a responsive landlord, owning rentals is not worth your time and money. Some properties also are not as good rentals as others.

There are some pitfalls regarding the sale of your fix-and-flip asset. The first pitfall is the FHA ninety-day flip rule. You have to have owned your house for ninety days before you can accept an FHA loan. Also, since you are selling the house retail, the odds are that you will have to go through a home inspection contingency. Rarely have I ever seen this be nothing, and even our nicest houses generate demands for a few thousand dollars in repairs (some fair, some not, but generally necessary).

Another huge pitfall is the appraisers. When selling your asset, odds are the purchaser will require a loan to acquire the property. This loan will require an appraiser. I cannot tell you how many times an appraiser has under-appraised our house because they are lazy, an out-of-town appraiser who does not know the market, or they are fixated on some feature as being critical to the valuation. When we sell fix-and-flip houses, we provide the appraiser with an appraisal package consisting of the most recent comps, a sales contract, and a detailed list of our renovations. Trying to send this information as an appeal *after* an appraisal seldom works unless you can point to a glaring error. Nobody likes to admit a mistake, but giving them the information in advance can help prevent one from ever happening.

There are also purchase location and condition pitfalls that can have a bigger impact on value for more people than you might expect. We avoid purchasing properties near heavily traveled roads, huge power lines, and railroad tracks. The difference in the perceived value of the exact same house one or two streets back can be huge. We have turned down many deals that have these characteristics.

Also, be careful if you are buying houses built before 1960. These houses could need considerable work, have outdated floor plans, contain solid aluminum wiring, two-pronged outlets, have lead paint, and the list goes on and on. We also avoid properties with black mold, asbestos, and vacant houses on septic systems. If a house is on a septic system and the house has been vacant for a year or more the odds are that the septic system needs major repairs or replacement.

While you are new to buying properties, it is a good idea to talk to a contractor, a realtor, or a fix-and-flip investor, or all three, about the type and location of the property you are considering. If you said, “Hey Ed, what do you think of a late 1960s or early 1970s-era ranch in North Springfield?” Ed would say how much he loves those properties. They are built solid as a rock, are inexpensive to renovate, sell fast as starter houses, and rent well in a good commuter location. However, Ed also would tell you they all have Orangeburg pipe to the sewer so make sure there is a certificate showing it was replaced or budget $50,000 or more to do so.

Key Takeaways:

You should have answers to all of these questions before you begin your flip.

- Be confident in your own pricing and don’t follow the herd.
- Decide how you are going to execute a flip. Are you hiring a contractor or are you subcontracting the work out yourself?
- Ask yourself, who is going to sell the house when it is done? How will the staging be handled?
- Understand your renovation and purchasing pitfalls.
- Do well by doing good.

Part 4

PUTTING IT ALL TOGETHER: TURNING YOUR CAPITAL STACK INTO PASSIVE AND RESIDUAL INCOME

"If you don't find a way to make money while you sleep, you will work until you die."
—Warren Buffett

You made it! You inherited a ton of money and can skip parts one, two, and three of this book and go right to passive investing so you can sip piña coladas in Bali. More likely, you are making some good active real estate investments, you have a good capital stack to pursue additional active projects, and you want to take some chips off the table and put some of your money to work for you with less risk and less effort on your part. This part of the book is also for you. As you want to move away from active efforts, you can shift more and more of your capital stack into passive efforts you learn here. Even before that, you can leverage your passive efforts to raise money for active efforts if you are so inclined. Everyone needs to understand the full roadmap to consider what they are working toward and their options along the way. So, keep reading and dream big even if you are starting with zero dollars.

Chapter 12
RESIDENTIAL RENTAL PORTFOLIO

"A neurotic is a man who builds a castle in the air. A psychotic is the man who lives in it. A psychiatrist is the man who collects the rent."
—Jerome Lawrence

The Power of a Rental Portfolio

Why do you want to own a rental portfolio? Do you really want to involve yourself with tenant screening, rent collection, and property maintenance? There is an upside! It is the power of the rental portfolio. Once you have the rental portfolio performing year over year, you have a relatively reliable income stream that you can leverage into more active real estate investments. How do I know? I know because we built a huge private lending business based on leveraging the "dead equity" of our rental portfolio. Even better, if and when we want to pull back, a rental portfolio is something we can sell entirely or hire someone to manage for us while we are on our beach in Bali.

How did we get started with rentals? We bought them! That's the easy part. What's a lot harder than buying rentals is finding them and financing them. That brings the subject back to finding the money. Make sure that you have the money lined up before you find a deal. Once you find a deal you will want to think fast and move fast to get it closed. You don't want any financing contingencies holding you up.

What does a performing rental portfolio look like? It looks just like a successful standalone business. You should put together a balance sheet as well as a profit and loss sheet for your rental portfolio. When you are starting out, you can prepare your own balance sheet as well as your profit and loss. Your balance sheet is going to show all of your liabilities (debts and bills you owe) and all of your assets. If you produce one that is just for your rental portfolio your assets will be the properties that you own and your liabilities will be the mortgages associated with them. When you subtract the liabilities from the assets you will have a net number that shows the value of your portfolio. For example, if you have three houses worth $250,000 each you have total assets of $750,000. If the loans on all three properties total $500,000, then the net value of your portfolio is $250,000. However, once those properties appreciate substantially you can borrow against the equity of the portfolio.

In this example, assume that your portfolio appreciates 6.5 percent a year for five years. At the end of five years, your assets will be worth $1,027,565! In that same period, if your loan includes a monthly principal payment, you will have reduced the amount due on your loan; perhaps you have paid it down to $450,000 in principal balance. If that is the case, you now have a portfolio with a net value of $577,565. If you go back to the bank and replace your loan with a 75 percent loan to value product– you can refinance the $450,000 loan with a $770,673.00 loan and take the difference of $320,673 out as cash in the bank to be used for the purchase of additional investments!

Tax Implications

Do people who have a lot of real estate and rental properties pay a lot of taxes? Maybe you've heard about rich politicians and investors who don't pay taxes because they have losses on real estate investments. Are they really losing money at business, not paying taxes, and making lots of money at the same time? These issues have become confusing due to rumors, bad information, and incomplete news reporting. Let's see if we can sort out some of this.

When you own a real estate asset you can depreciate it. Depreciation is the process of writing off some portion of the investment every year to reflect its decreasing value over time. Depreciation is a tax deduction that reduces your taxable income and therefore your tax liability. However, it is important to note that depreciation is a paper loss and does not actually reduce your cash flow. This means that even if you have a positive cash flow from your rental properties, you may still be able to show a loss on your tax return due to depreciation.

The amount of depreciation you can claim each year is based on the value of the property, the cost of any improvements, and the useful life of the property. For residential rental properties, the useful life is generally twenty-seven and a half years. This means that you can deduct 3.63 percent (1/27th) of the property's value each year for twenty-seven and a half years. For example, if you have a rental property worth $350,000, you can deduct $12,727.27 per year in depreciation ($350,000 divided by 27.5).

Depreciation is just one of the many tax benefits of owning real estate. Other tax benefits include mortgage interest deductions (if your real estate is a primary or second residence), property tax deductions, and the ability to defer capital gains taxes through a 1031 exchange for a like property. However, it is important to consult with a tax professional to ensure that you are taking advantage of all the tax benefits available to you and that you are accurately reporting your rental income and expenses.

In summary, while it is true that real estate investors can use depreciation to reduce their tax liability, it is not a loophole or a way to avoid paying taxes altogether. Depreciation is a legitimate tax deduction that reflects the decreasing value of a rental property over time. However, it is important to understand the rules and limitations surrounding depreciation and to work with a tax professional to ensure that you are accurately reporting your rental income and expenses.

Once we owned about fifty rental properties, we found a very nice tax benefit called a cost segregation study. This was a tax study of all our assets that separated out the building components, such as electrical and plumbing systems, roof, and HVAC systems, from the building structure. The benefit of this study was that it allowed us to accelerate the depreciation of the building components, which are typically shorter-lived assets, and claim more tax deductions in the earlier years of ownership. By doing this, we were able to significantly reduce our tax liability and increase our cash flow. However, it's important to note that a cost segregation study can be a complex process and requires the expertise of a qualified professional, such as a tax accountant or engineer. The cost of the study can also vary depending on the size and complexity of the property, but the potential tax benefits can be significant, especially for investors with a large portfolio of rental properties. Overall, a cost segregation study is just one example of how real estate investors can take advantage of the tax benefits of owning rental properties and maximize their returns. The cost segregation study is a great savings tool to use in years when you owe a lot of taxes. The downside of it is that you pump a lot of depreciation out of your assets that you can't use in later years.

Now for the downside of depreciation. What happens to your tax situation when you sell a fully depreciated asset? Uh oh! Now, you owe a *lot* of taxes. When you sell a fully depreciated asset, you will owe capital gains taxes on the sale. The reason for this is that depreciation reduces the cost basis of the property, which is used to calculate the gain or loss on the sale. The gain is the difference between the sale price and the adjusted basis, which includes the original cost of the property minus any depreciation taken. Because the depreciation reduces the adjusted basis, the gain on the sale will be higher, which means you will owe more in taxes.

However, there are ways to minimize the tax impact of selling a fully depreciated asset. One option is to do a 1031 exchange, which allows you to defer the capital gains taxes on the sale by reinvesting the proceeds in a similar property. Another option is to donate the property to a charity or do a charitable remainder trust, which can provide tax benefits while also supporting a good cause.

Appreciation

Are you a believer in the long-term growth of real estate values? If you are a student of history, you will learn that real estate has been one of the most reliable long-term investments over time. According to the

National Association of Realtors, the median price of existing homes in the United States has increased by an average of 5.4 percent annually since 1968. That means a $100,000 home in 1968 would be worth over $500,000 today. Of course, there have been periods of ups and downs, but over the long term, real estate has generally outperformed inflation and provided a stable source of wealth for many investors.

One of the reasons for the long-term growth of real estate values is the simple fact of supply and demand. As the population grows and urbanizes, the demand for housing increases, which puts upward pressure on prices. In addition, real estate is a tangible asset that can provide both rental income and potential appreciation, making it an attractive investment option for many people.

Your real estate holdings are held long-term. If you lock in a good long-term rate, you can control your monthly interest expenses. Unfortunately, you won't be able to control the cost of repairs, taxes, and insurance. However, increasing costs are generally more than offset by the cost of rent. Why do properties keep appreciating? The cost to replace them keeps increasing. When local governments provide thorough oversight of the development process, they find that product quality can improve but it costs a lot more to deliver the product. Long planning cycles and regulatory oversight of construction materials drive up costs. This means replacing your existing product is more expensive than it was to build it. The utility of the housing product remains approximately the same, so the cost of existing housing inventory continues to go up.

Overall, real estate is a complex and dynamic asset class that requires careful consideration and planning. However, for those who are willing to put in the effort and take a long-term perspective, real estate can be a powerful tool for building wealth and achieving financial security. By locking in a good long-term interest rate and managing your expenses effectively, you can position yourself for success in the real estate market.

Purchase Rules and Rental Plans

You are going to need some general rules to help you figure out what kind of assets to put in your portfolio. Here are some of the best guidelines that we have used.

When building a real estate portfolio, it's important to establish guidelines that can help you make informed decisions about which assets to invest in. These guidelines should be based on a variety of factors, such as the physical nature of the assets, the location of the properties, and the rental ratios of the properties.

One important consideration is to buy assets that are similar in physical nature, as this can make it easier to manage repairs and maintenance between properties. For example, if you invest in properties that have similar HVAC systems or plumbing, you can use the same repair and maintenance crews for all of your properties, which can save time and money. Similarly, if you invest in properties with similar layouts, you can standardize the renovations and upgrades you make to each property, which can help you streamline the process and reduce costs.

Another important factor to consider is the location of the properties. It's generally best to invest in properties that are geographically close to where you live so that you can provide direct oversight of repairs and maintenance, as well as meet with tenants as needed. This can help you build better relationships with your tenants and ensure that your properties are being well-maintained. Additionally, investing in properties that are close to your primary residence can help you save time and money on travel expenses.

When considering potential properties, it's also important to evaluate the rent ratios of the properties. Rent ratios are the ratio of rent to purchase price, and can help you determine whether a property is a good investment. For example, you may want to set a ratio of rent to purchase price for the area where you are investing, such as 1 percent. This means that you would buy a property when the purchase price is equal to or lower than 100 times the rent. By setting these criteria in advance, you can help ensure that you are investing in properties that are likely to generate a good return on investment.

Finally, when making purchase decisions, it's important to remember that no amount of discount on appliances can make up for a bad purchase decision. This means that you need to carefully evaluate potential properties and avoid overpaying for a property or investing in one that has too few bedrooms to make it a desirable rental. By making informed and thoughtful decisions, you can build a successful and profitable real estate portfolio that can help you achieve your financial goals.

Financing the Assets Long Term

When you acquire an asset, you can afford to spend a bit of extra money on a hard money loan to fix it and get it performing. This is especially the case if you have found a good asset at a good buy price. However, the success of your long-term portfolio is going to largely relate to the cost of ownership. Financing is a big part of ownership costs. If you are putting together a small portfolio of homes, you will be able to get conventional financing from a bank. This can create excellent value and provide you with access to long-term, low-cost funds. However, once you own more than ten mortgages, you are going to need to get something other than conventional financing. That leaves you with a choice between cash purchases and bank financing. Cash ownership is easy to understand, but you miss out on all the benefits of leverage and are limited as to what you can purchase by the finite amount of cash you have on hand. Then, there is community bank financing that generally has a reset of the interest rate every five years. Once you are pursuing community bank financing you will find out that they are going to do a deep dive into your financial position. They will make sure that you have adequate insurance on your assets and they will look at your total net worth, income, personal insurance, expenses, and creditworthiness.

The process of getting a community bank loan gets harder when you have a bigger portfolio. Each decision-maker in the community bank needs to be able to understand your total financial picture. If you have a lot of assets, multiple entities, or multiple business partners–figuring out your financial picture is going to be a challenge for a community bank. This is not to say that it isn't worth the effort. Just plan on taking about five times longer than you would expect the process to take. This was the case for the last portfolio loan we secured. It took ten months from start to finish to lock the interest rate and close the loan. A lot can happen to interest rates in this period. I hope for you that they go down, but in the real world, interest rates go in both directions. A couple of points on interest rate expenditures can significantly change the financial viability of your real estate projects.

Managing the Assets (Asset Maintenance, Rent Collection)

Managing rental properties involves a variety of tasks, such as maintaining the properties, collecting rent, and responding to tenant requests. Once you have identified potential properties, it's important to have a strategy for getting them into good rental condition. This can involve making renovations or upgrades to the properties, such as installing new appliances or updating the electrical or plumbing systems. However, it's important to strike a balance between investing in the properties and over-investing in them. One strategy is to improve the properties to the point where they are in good condition and require only periodic maintenance, but are not troubled by chronic problems. This can help avoid the high costs associated with chronic repairs and vacancies.

Another key aspect of managing rental properties is determining how to handle repair and maintenance requests. It's important to be responsive to your tenants' needs and to address material defects in the property or equipment as quickly as possible. This not only shows respect for your tenants but can also help prevent small problems from becoming major expenses. Additionally, if you live in a climate with extreme temperatures, it's important to be especially responsive to HVAC-related issues to ensure that your tenants are comfortable and healthy.

To facilitate responsive repairs and maintenance, it's important to have a team of skilled professionals who can handle different types of repairs. This may include an HVAC technician, an electrician, a plumber, and a handyman, all of whom should be able to show up within twenty-four hours of a tenant's request. It's also important to choose professionals who can work efficiently and respectfully, entering the property without making a mess or disturbing the tenants. By having a team of reliable professionals in place, you can minimize repair costs and improve the rental experience for your tenants.

Finally, to maximize tenant satisfaction and reduce turnover, it's important to maintain good relationships with your tenants. This can involve regular communication, promptly responding to tenant requests, and treating your tenants with respect and professionalism. By building trust and loyalty with your tenants, you can help ensure that they renew their leases and remain in your properties long-term. Ultimately, effective asset maintenance and rent collection strategies are crucial for building a successful and profitable real estate portfolio.

By focusing on these key takeaways and investing in the right team and resources, you can maximize your returns and achieve your financial goals

Key Takeaways

- Building a rental portfolio is a great way to build positive cash flow and wealth by taking advantage of market appreciation and principal paydown through rent.
- Buy similar assets in close proximity.
- Use the 100-times-rent rule as a pricing guide to buy rentals.
- Maintain good tenant relations for longer-term tenants.
- Rentals are a good tax strategy by taking advantage of tax depreciation.

Chapter 13

PURCHASING COMMERCIAL REAL ESTATE

"Landlords grow rich in their sleep without working. . . ."
—John Stuart Mill

Investing in commercial real estate offers another path to creating passive and/or active income. Entire books have been written on this topic. We wanted to cover some basic concepts so you can consider what other options for real estate investing exist once you have built up your capital stack. One of the biggest advantages of commercial real estate is attractive leasing rates and longer lease contracts. It also offers the potential for long-term capital appreciation. Structuring leasing to place the burden of paying taxes and improving or maintaining the property entirely on the tenant through an "NNN lease" (to be discussed) is one very common option that allows you as the owner to passively sit back and watch the income roll.

Commercial real estate is property that is used for business purposes. However, certain types of commercial real estate are used as residences such as apartment buildings or trailer parks. Commercial real estate is primarily leased to tenants conducting income-producing activities. Types of commercial real estate include shopping malls, strip centers, office buildings (including medical), hotels, apartment buildings, self-storage, industrial (warehouse, mixed-use, industrial storage), raw land, and trailer parks. I might have missed a few but you get the idea.

Individuals and companies can make money from commercial real estate by holding (occupying property with a business you own), leasing (to others), developing and leasing (to others), developing and selling, and redeveloping (changing the use of the property). In our careers, we have done four of the five strategies. We have not occupied a commercial property that we own with a business that we own. (Well, we did own that car wash and the land it sat on, but it was only a short time before the government bulldozed it for an on-ramp.) While in the real estate business, we have only worked from home! Our staff has done likewise since long before the pandemic, which they enjoy as a benefit and we enjoy by not paying to lease office space.

Financing commercial real estate works differently than residential home purchases. Banks and investors evaluate commercial real estate based on capitalization rates. In chapter five, we talked about capitalization rates (CAP), which is the ratio of net operating income (NOI) to property asset value. It is stated in terms of a percentage. Simply put, the CAP rate is used to calculate the value of income-producing properties. This is a guide for helping investors analyze if the property is a good deal or not. For example, if you have a trailer park that is a lot for rent-only (do not own trailers), good condition, and fully leased parks are selling for a 5 CAP (5 percent return on your money). If you have the chance to buy this kind of asset at a 10 CAP, this could be a good deal. Keep in mind you will have to take into consideration other factors of the deal such as the location of the site, how many rentable lots, and/or the condition of the infrastructure (water, sewer, storm management, and/or roads). Understanding the CAP rate of an asset can help you quickly determine if the asset is overpriced.

Another concept you need to understand in commercial space is zoning. Zoning is based on local laws (city, county, parishes) that govern how real estate property can be used. Zoning laws can limit and prevent what happens in a particular area. Local governments/municipalities partition districts and neighborhoods to define what can happen in that specific area. Some examples of zoning include single-family residential, multifamily residential, heavy industrial, light industrial, manufacturing, business, and/or agricultural designations. There are different subcategories for each type of zoning.

In most jurisdictions, the zoning codes are represented by letters. Typically, "R" is used to designate residential. There are usually subcategories of residential: R-1, R-2, R-4, R-8, etc. In some cases, an R-2 could mean that you could build two houses on an acre of land. Keep in mind that this is not one size fits all. Each local government has different definitions of their letters. You need to research the zoning regulations in your area and determine what the authorized zoning use is of the land.

Each jurisdiction typically has a document called the "Master Plan" that includes zoning codes, and a Code of Ordinances, all of which can include rules about the commercial use of land. These documents commonly can be found in the local zoning and planning office or through a quick online search. You can certainly get a good sense of what generally is intended to be allowed and disallowed in a given area. However, zoning can vary enormously depending on what a particular locale might want and there can be many nuances sprinkled throughout these documents and other laws and regulations that could cause you all sorts of problems. I would hire a land use attorney to research a parcel in detail because the permitted (or banned) uses can make an enormous impact on the short-term and long-term value of each commercial property.

One key concept you should know about (and will see throughout most zoning rules) is the term " by right use." This relates to the fact that when you purchase a property you are held bound to the current zoning of the property. The "by right" is the pre-authorized legal use of the land. For example, if you purchase a property that is designated with an "R" (residential), you cannot put a shopping mall or warehouse on this property. Now, let's say you buy two acres of land that is R-4 (in our case four houses per acre). You can subdivide the land to get eight, one-quarter-acre lots to build eight houses. Simple math but infrastructure such as roads, curbs, and utilities will bring this number down to six or seven. Hopefully, you get the idea.

I will note in passing that there are sometimes ways to go beyond the by-right use by seeking and obtaining a variance from a jurisdiction's zoning authorities. Perhaps our piece of land zoned R-4 to serve as an example, is a few dozen square feet under two acres or the building setbacks are twenty-five feet, but you need to go within twenty feet of the property line to fit the four properties desired. Or perhaps the R-4 is next to a commercial area, and you'd like to get the land rezoned for a warehouse. In most jurisdictions, you can request a variance to waive or modify many if not all zoning rules. However, the process, no matter how simple or reasonable the request might seem to you, is almost always time-consuming, expensive, and uncertain in outcome because it usually is at the discretion of a zoning board.

The primary reason I even raise the variance option is so that you don't evaluate a property and value it assuming you can get a variance because even a very simple one can be hard to get. Don't give into the siren song of a seller who has an incentive to tell you it will be easy for you to get approval for anything. Make value decisions based on the by-right uses and if you need to go beyond that value, consult a land-use attorney familiar with that locality. That said, if you see a profit in buying and using a property by right, there might be a lot of value to be unleashed by spending the time and money to seek and obtain a variance for a higher value use.

There are many types of commercial assets. Below are the types of commercial assets that we will cover in this book. We will define each one, and cover investment strategies, and finance options. All of the property types below can be used as income-producing. We have experience with most of them.

Below are the types we will cover:

1. Industrial/Manufacturing (warehouse, mixed-use, industrial storage)
2. Trailer Parks
3. Raw Land
4. Self-Storage Facilities
5. Office Buildings (Class A, Class B, Class C, and medical)

6. Shopping Centers
7. Hotels
8. Apartment Buildings

Industrial/Manufacturing

Industrial properties can be raw or improved land or buildings used for storage, manufacturing, research and development, production, maintenance, and distribution of goods. Industrial property often can also include office space. This is called a mixed-use development. The most common types of industrial property are:

- Heavy/Light Manufacturing
- Warehouse and Distribution
- Cold Storage
- Flex Space or Mixed Use
- Data Centers
- Showrooms
- Truck/Heavy Equipment Storage Lots
- Research and Development

Investors are attracted to the industrial asset class because of the high-rent demand and the consistent stable, long-term returns. Another reason that investors want industrial real estate is that very few jurisdictions with dense development are approving any new industrial sites. Attempts to get variances will usually be met by public disapproval and political pushback, making them extremely hard to obtain. This leads to less supply and more demand which means the assets go up in value.

Some investment strategies include:

1) Buy industrial land on the outskirts of a city/metropolitan near a railroad tie, highway, or transportation center.

2) Buy a single piece of land with the intent of making it a truck yard or heavy equipment storage lot (less development costs than a warehouse).

3) Buy property near a future redevelopment center.

4) Buy a property where you can develop it into a warehouse or flex space. Flex space appeals to a wider tenant mix which reduces the vacancy rate of the property.

One of our most successful investments was the purchase of a three-acre piece of industrial property near an airport. The lot was flat and rectangular. A good friend of ours found a piece of industrial property but did not have the resources to buy it himself. So, he approached us to help him buy it. I thought he just wanted a hard money loan so he could buy it himself. That was not the case. He wanted us to own the property collectively, to which we said yes. His idea was to convert the property into a semi-truck storage lot and collect what is called space rents.

Even though we did not have experience in operating a truck yard, I felt comfortable because we owned so many residential rentals that this would be a good transition into another asset class. Another advantage to this site is that we did not have to do much development work. We just had to lay asphalt millings (a cheaper form of pavement), construct a perimeter fence, and set up each individual lot. We also had to pay for engineers and such for a site plan. The purchase price of the parcel was $1,325,000 of which we had to put down about $400,000. The layout of the actual site had a bunch of parking sites of different sizes for different trucks. However, the most common parking is for semi-tractor trailers. The average price per spot is $350 per space and we have approximately seventy-eight spaces. Our average monthly income generated from this truck yard is about $27,500 a month. Our expenses include property taxes, utilities, property management, and minimal maintenance. For simplicity's sake, our monthly expenses totaled about $2,500 leaving us with a monthly NOI of $25,000 a month. Now, this property is evaluated based on consistent NOI. These industrial truck yards sell around a 5 CAP. If you do the cap rate math on this property, the current value of it is $25,000 x 12 months = $300,000 per year income. $300,000 / 0.05 (5 CAP) = $6,000,000.

Trailer Parks

A trailer park, mobile home park, or manufactured home community, is an area for mobile homes and travel trailers. These can be either permanent or temporary areas. There are also RV lots which are different but not part of this discussion. The advantages of these parks are the low cost of housing compared to other housing. Owning a trailer park is a great cash-flowing investment if you get it at a fair price.

There are two different business models related to the ownership of a trailer park. One option is when you own a trailer park where the tenants own their own homes and pay only lot rent. Lot rent is where the owner of the trailer pays the owner of the trailer park rent to occupy a single pad site. You can also own a park where you own the land and the trailers. I am not a fan of this model as it has a big maintenance component on the individual trailers which impacts cash flow.

Some investment strategies include:

- Buy a trailer park, lot rents only, at a 9 CAP or more with limited vacancies.
- Buy a trailer park, lot rents only, with a lot of vacancies but in a good location for a good price.
- Buy a park where you own the trailers for a great price, convert the trailers with owner financing, and have the tenants become owners of their trailers. This might be easier said than done because of the tenant's ability to pay.
- Buy a piece of land that can be converted into the correct zoning for a trailer park and build out your own infrastructure. Keep in mind that many local jurisdictions will not allow this as they do not want any of these communities in their backyard.
- Buy a dilapidated trailer park that needs infrastructure improvement such as roads, water, sewer, and stormwater management upgrades. When complete, raise the lot rents.

Being in real estate, I come across many investment opportunities. I happen to also be president of a nonprofit that is in the affordable housing space. There was a trailer park in the City of Manassas where the owners died and left it in a trust for a special needs adult child (autistic). The trailer park was in a trust handled by a lawyer who knew nothing about maintaining trailer parks. The park became very dilapidated and, believe it or not, had excrement coming out of the sewer pipes along with other atrocities. The city made an offer to the trust and was going to buy the trailer park and condemn it. This would have forced more than fifty households to find new housing. I was called by another nonprofit to see if we could help relocate these households. I said that we could not because there was nowhere for these people to go to match their financial situation. Instead, I said, "Why don't we just buy it?"

The problem with "just buying" the trailer park was my nonprofit was running in the red and had no money to buy it. If you've learned anything from this book, it should be that having no money should not stop you. Therefore, I put together a pro forma to see if the nonprofit could afford the park by purchasing it and putting in the new infrastructure. Once I understood the monthly cash flow, I had a better understanding of the debt we could take on to both purchase the park and repair or replace the infrastructure (water pipes, sewer system, storm management system, and new roads).

You are probably wondering how a nonprofit could pull this off. Well, as people tell me, "You must have been lucky." Yep. I must have been. Next, I met with the lawyer handling the trust and asked him how much the special needs child required per month to survive. He told me $10,000 a month. I asked him if the trust would hold seller financing. He said yes. I got the trust to agree to hold a seller-financed first trust for $1,400,000 at 3.5 percent interest on a fifteen-year amortization schedule. Guess what the payment was? $10,010.

Next, I had the problem of getting the infrastructure redeveloped. This is where I was lucky. My nonprofit had a board member, Daniel Woodward, who owned a construction company and he agreed to do the work, about $1,000,000, in return for a second trust position. I was off to the races. So, in total, we were all in for $2,400,000. At the time the average rents were below $650 a month but we had to raise them. Below is the pro forma that I put together to afford the park.

Pro Forma			
Revenues	**Year 1**	**Year 2**	**Year 3**
Leased Lots (58 total)	49	53	56
Average Rent Per Space	$650	$650	$650
Income on Paid Rent	$382,200	$413,400	$436,800
Water/Sewer ($50/lot/mon	$29,400	$0	$0
Extra (pet fee/vending)			
Other (late fees, fines, etc)	$3,000	$3,600	$3,960
Total Income	$414,600	$417,000	$440,760
Expenses			
Real Estate Taxes	$26,000	$26,520	$27,050
Insurance	$5,000	$5,100	$5,202
Utilities (water/sewer)	$72,000	$5,000	$5,100
Marketing/Legal	$1,000	$3,000	$3,090
Office Supplies	$500	$510	$520
Property Management - 5%	$22,932	$24,804	$26,208
Maintenance - 6%	$6,000	$6,120	$6,242
Total Expenses	$133,432	$71,054	$73,412
(expenses as % income)	32%	17%	17%
Net Operating Income	$281,168	$345,946	$367,348
Debt Service			
Loan Pay $1.4MM	$120,120	$120,120	$120,120
3.5% - 15 Year ARM			
Loan Pay (Rehab) $983M			
5.0% - 25 Year ARM	$93,348	$93,348	$93,348
Total Debt Service	$213,468	$213,468	$213,468
TOTAL CASH FLOW	$67,700	$132,478	$153,879

This is a monthly snapshot of the park today and what it is worth given a particular cap rate.

Cash Flow Statement Manassas Trailer Park (Full Debt Service)

Monthly Cash Flow Trailer Park (Full Debt Service)		
INCOME		Monthly
Assertion Pad Sites (49 @ $700/mo)		$34,300
Non Assertion Pad Sites (1 @ $725/mo)		$725
Non Assertion Pad Sites (6 @ $750/mo)		$4,500
Late Fees (Blended) (2 @ $67.50/mo)		$135
Total Gross Income		$39,660
EXPENSES		
Real Estate Taxes ($22,987/yr)		$1,916
Maintenance (Trees/Snow)		$500
Water/Sewer (Small Building)		$20
Electric (Property Lights)		$179
Insurance		$230
Total Expenses		$2,845
Operating Income		$36,815
Debt Service		
Acquisition Debt Service		$9,937
Rehab Debt Service		$7,600
Total Debt Service		$17,537
Total Expenses		$20,382
Cash Flow		$19,278
Value of the trailer park at various CAP rates:		
	10 cap	$4,417,800
	9 cap	$4,908,667
	8 cap	$5,522,250
	7 cap	$6,311,143
	6.75 cap	$6,544,889
	5.5 cap	$8,032,364
	5 cap	$8,835,600
	4.8 cap	$9,203,750
	4.5 cap	$9,817,333

Raw Land

Raw land is exactly what it sounds like. It is a plot of land that has not been developed or prepared for construction. It has a specific zoning attached to it, usually agriculture or residential. However, there could be other zoning types attached as well; like industrial or commercial. Raw land can be income-producing. It could be leased for agriculture/farming purposes, mineral rights, trees, etc. There are many advantages associated with raw land investment. Raw land can be easy to acquire, has the possibility of little or no competition, is low cost to maintain, has the potential for a quick profit, and can generate passive income.

Some investment strategies include:

1) Buy land on the outskirts of a city/metropolitan area and hold for many years waiting for urban sprawl.

2) Buy a single plot with the correct zoning use and subdivide it into smaller lots to increase the value.

3) Develop buildings on the land to increase its value.

4) Lease the land.

Financing raw land can be challenging, typically, because it can't be put to economic use without improvement or at least a lease in the future, which can make its valuation seem a bit speculative. You can buy land with cash, of course, bank loans (more than likely from community banks), and hard money lenders. The maximum loan terms from a bank typically are ten years or less and based on an extremely conservative valuation of the property based on by-right uses. Most banks will make you put up a 50 percent down payment. Banks see land loans as very risky loans. Hard money lenders will be more aggressive in their pricing and terms depending on the subdivision or other capability and the by-right income-producing aspect of the land.

On a few occasions, we have taken a piece of raw land and subdivided the land into four or five lots for a housing development. Once we finished subdividing the land, we got a new site plan defining the new lots, road/curb cuts, and where the utilities would go. We took that site plan and simply sold it to a builder. You might think it is a good idea to build houses on the land and sell them. That is beyond the scope of the real estate investor and moves you into a home builder–which is a totally different business.

Self-Storage

Self-storage is what individuals and businesses use to store their extra belongings and assets. They might not have enough current space to store these items, so they need to get more space. Given the high demand for space to store household belongings and/or business equipment, self-storage facilities have become very popular.

This is a solid investment for several reasons. These assets have high earning potential. Storage units cost less than commercial buildings and residential real estate. Demand is growing as the baby boomers are downsizing.

The business is simple to operate. The storage property owner charges customers rent to store their belongings. These spaces come in different sizes/prices depending on what the customer needs. Some sites can also store vehicles.

There are four types of self-storage facilities: climate-controlled, drive-up/outdoor storage, mixed-use storage, and vehicle storage. These types have their advantages and disadvantages. The drive-up facility is the most affordable and the customer has complete access to their unit. This facility requires minimal maintenance and employees. Climate-controlled storage is the most expensive. These facilities are used for storing art, furniture, and musical instruments that benefit from climate control. Vehicle storage is ideal for those searching for a sheltered, locked parking lot. We own a vehicle storage, but it is not sheltered. It is only for commercial vehicles, not for cars or boats.

There are four primary ways to invest in self-storage space.

1) Buy an existing facility. At this point, you are armed with the skills to determine if the facility is a good deal or not by analyzing the NOI and determining what CAP rate you want to purchase it for.

2) Develop your own facility. This is not easy but might be the best route. You need to purchase land preferably that is already zoned for this use (by right). Manage the construction, etc.

3) Invest in a publicly traded storage business (stock market).

4) **Best case for passive income: purchase shares in a real estate investment trust** that specializes in storage units across the country.

Office Buildings

An office building is a property that is used as a place of business for office workers. This category has four subtypes: Class A, Class B, Class C, and Medical. Class A office buildings represent the best buildings in terms of age, quality of infrastructure, and location. Class B buildings are older than Class A and not as competitive price-wise. Investors usually target these buildings for restoration. Class C buildings are usually twenty years and older, located in less attractive areas, and in need of maintenance. The last type of office buildings are buildings for medical purposes. Usually, you will find a lot of these buildings centrally located near a hospital. These properties are owned and leased out to tenants. They are not used as residences.

Office buildings are leased out with commercial leases. Commercial leases typically run from one year to ten years or more. The lease term might be for twenty years but has four five-year terms. A commercial real estate lawyer versed in this subject matter is usually needed for these leases. There are four types of leases with different levels of tenant/landlord responsibility.

1) A **gross lease** is where the tenant only pays the rent. The landlord pays for the property taxes, insurance, and maintenance.

2) A **single net lease** has the tenant paying the rent and property taxes. The landlord pays for insurance and maintenance.

3) A **double net lease** makes the tenant responsible for rent, taxes, and insurance. The landlord pays for maintenance.

4) A **triple net lease (NNN)** has the tenant paying all four costs. A lease is priced out as dollars per square foot. This quote is on an annual basis. For example, if I have a 20,000-square-foot space that I rent for $15 a square foot what is my monthly rent? I am assuming a gross lease. The answer is 20,000 x $15.00 / 12 = $25,000 a month. An NNN lease is an excellent way to generate the most passive form of income. Make the tenant do everything and you collect the rent.

How do I calculate the NOI of this type of asset? This is simple. The income side consists of adding up all the monthly leases. Do you have paid parking? Are you renting the rooftop to any cellular companies, etc.? The expense side consists of maintenance costs, insurance, taxes, property management, possibly cleaning costs, etc. The result of this is your NOI. Keep in mind you do not include any debt service in this calculation.

Some investment strategies include:

1) Buy a building with strong tenants and long-term NNN leases at a good CAP rate and very few vacancies.

2) Buy a building at a great price with high vacancies for a good price.

3) Purchase an older outdated building and redevelop the land for its highest and best use.

Rarely are these buildings purchased with cash. Most mid-size buildings are financed through local community banks. However, the larger buildings are funded through the largest-sized banks. If a project is big then there could be participatory financing where different banks, insurance companies, and pension funds pitch in to fund the entire deal.

We have been writing this book for three years since the start of the COVID-19 pandemic. The pandemic had a detrimental impact on this asset class. More workers in both the private industry space and government have been working from home. This has resulted in a consolidation in the amount of workspace that is needed. As a result, companies need less office space. This has caused a domino effect throughout the country and will eventually impact the commercial banking sector. We suggest staying away from these assets until you can see the start of a turnaround. Of course, if you understand and can value the market, the availability of distressed assets could become very profitable.

Shopping Centers

A shopping center is a group of retail stores and service establishments catering to a community or neighborhood. It can also cater to a regional area. Shopping centers usually have plenty of parking. They are usually located in suburban areas but could be in downtown areas in more densely populated spaces. Shopping centers come in two different styles: mall and strip center. You are probably familiar with both structures. One is open air and the other is mainly indoors on two or three levels with stores facing each other and central walkways.

Shopping centers are leased out space by space. Each separate retail space (store) has its own square footage requirement. The largest spaces in a shopping center are called anchors. Anchors could be a grocery store or a large merchandising tenant such as Target, Macy's, Wal-Mart, etc. Shopping centers have three types of leases:

1) A **gross lease** is where the tenant only pays the rent. The landlord pays for the property taxes, insurance, and maintenance.

2) A **modified gross lease** has the tenant paying the rent and other expenses while the landlord pays for some other expenses as well. These terms are defined in the lease.

3) A **triple net lease (NNN)** is a favorite among landlords because the tenant pays the rent, and a pro-rata share of the property taxes, maintenance, and insurance. Leases are priced out as dollars per square foot. This cost per square foot is quoted on an annual basis.

Some investment strategies include:

1) Look for stabilized centers with a strong anchor(s) and good street appeal. Usually, shopping centers with well-established grocery stores are best because people will frequent them two or three times a week.

2) Buy a shopping center with multiple stores and tenants in an area(s) with strong income and high population growth.

3) Occupancy should be 80 percent or better with long-term leases.

4) Purchase the shopping center below its replacement cost.

5) Buy older shopping centers with the intent to repurpose the land for a higher density use on the land.

Keep in mind that e-tailing (shopping on the Internet) has impacted this asset class. Some call it the "Amazon effect." I generally would avoid buying shopping malls as a lot of them are going out of business across the country and the future use of these properties with e-tailing is unclear. Many of these assets need to be repurposed, but that could involve the uncertain process of seeking rezoning and extensive renovation costs. Local strip centers with well-established businesses, including restaurants, would be a good investment provided you do not overpay! As you can see, an important part of investing in commercial assets is to really understand the current economic and consumer trends.

Hotels

We all probably know what a hotel is, though services like Airbnb have stretched the concept more than a bit. We will talk here just about commercial properties used as hotels to provide short-term room rentals for guests. Key information on a hotel is the occupancy rate, which is a percentage of the available rooms. The average dollar-per-room of the occupied room or average daily rate is another key indicator. Hotel investing is a good way to diversify your portfolio. Hotels can deliver both short-term and long-term benefits. Hotels can generate income quickly provided the hotel is in a good area and the hotel is managed carefully.

There are five ways to invest in hotels:

1) Buy into hotel real estate investment trusts. This is a good passive income strategy.

2) Buy shares in a hotel operating company on the stock exchange.

3) Participate in a crowd-funded hotel investment, this could be in the form of syndication. You could participate with a lower amount of investment dollars in a crowd-funded model than any other model.

4) Purchase an existing hotel, again analyzing the NOI.

5) Build a new hotel. The last two strategies will involve a lot of planning and capital.

Successful strategies for hotel investments include:

- **Research the location and environment.** A hotel located in a thriving business center could be ideal. Is there shopping close by? How much land is available for other hotels? What are the occupancy rates of the nearby hotels?
- **Research the hotel's finances.** Look at the NOI. Is there growth potential? How is the hotel performing? What is the value of the hotel?
- **Keep in mind that the hotel is part of the service industry and not just a brick-and-mortar business.** You must evaluate the quality and performance level of the staff and management.
- **Understand the reservation system.** Is it part of a bigger hotel chain? Can the system be improved?

Apartment Buildings

Investing in apartments is another good way to build wealth, create passive income, and diversify your portfolio. By the time you are ready to invest here, you will know a lot about the local residential real estate rental market and should find it relatively easy to grasp apartment fundamentals since they are very related.

There are four different classes of apartments: Class A, Class B, Class C, and Class D. Class A apartments are usually newer and offer high-end amenities like fitness centers, yoga studios, clubhouses, and resort-style swimming pools. They are in desirable locations such as central high-traffic hubs, work locations, and shopping centers. Tenants in these communities have higher incomes and can afford to pay more rent.

Class B buildings are older (fifteen to twenty years) than Class A and not as competitive price-wise. They do not offer the same amenities. These properties are in a good neighborhood and are made up of working-class tenants seeking a cheaper alternative than Class A.

Class C buildings are older buildings, located in less attractive areas and need significant repairs and upgrades. The upside is that these properties tend to cost less upfront and can be a fantastic investment opportunity. However, they bring a greater risk of tenant turnover. As in commercial office space, residential apartment rents per square foot are cheaper the further into the alphabet you go.

Class D apartments are considered distressed properties. These properties are either abandoned or have been neglected by their owner. These projects will need a lot of time and money to get them in a performing status.

The net operating income of an apartment is simple in terms of the elements that make it up. The income side consists of the monthly income stream and late fees. The expenses side consists of property management, vacancies, turnover costs, ongoing maintenance, and attorney costs in case of an eviction.

There are four ways to invest in apartments:

1) Buy into a real estate investment trust (REIT). This is a good passive income strategy. A REIT is a large corporation that runs and manages many properties. In a REIT, you are buying shares in the REIT and not the property itself.

2) Buy an apartment yourself. This will be more capital intensive but analyzing whether it is a good deal or not should be simple. Again, analyze the NOI over a period of time.

3) Invest in a syndication. A syndication is a pooling of funds to purchase a property. Each syndication has an offering. There is a sponsor of the syndication (people putting it together). The sponsors are usually the general partner(s) making all the decisions and the investors are limited partners or passive investors.

4) Raise money and create your own syndication.

There are many ways to get started in the commercial real estate space. This is usually the most capital-intensive aspect of investing. If you invest in this space correctly it could only take one property to meet your monthly footprint, and that alone can make you financially free.

These key takeaways will help you further understand the commercial asset space.

Key Takeaways:

- Understand the zoning of the asset. What are the zoning and by-right uses?
- Understand how to correctly calculate the net operating income (NOI), if income-producing.
- Understand CAP rate and its relationship to value.
- Know whether this commercial asset can be repurposed for a higher and better use.
- Understand financing options for commercial assets.
- Understand trends in the overall marketplace to help you avoid bad asset decisions.

Chapter 14
TAX LIEN INVESTING

"While some people might find it distasteful to pay taxes, I don't. I find it patriotic."
—Mark Cuban

Death and taxes are inevitable. Why not profit from them when you can? This book is not about the funeral business (which apparently is very profitable), so let's talk about real estate taxes. We all pay them in some form if we own our home. If you buy and sell real estate, you will learn a great deal about property taxes as a cost that must be accounted for and reduces your profits.

What if I told you that, instead of only paying out real estate taxes, you can earn interest based on them as much as 18 percent or even 21 percent depending on the jurisdiction? (This number can end up much lower as we'll discuss). Buying tax liens is the method I will explain here, and it can be a great way to generate relatively passive and well-protected income. That said, there are some costly pitfalls to understand and carefully avoid so your investment is not wiped out.

You already know the basics of real estate tax, but let's consider them and their purpose in a little more detail so the intended functioning of tax liens is clear. Normally, a local governmental entity sets a real estate tax rate each year to collect enough money to cover the estimated budget for the next year of running that locality's operations, such as its schools, police and fire departments, road improvements, etc. Each property owner is then billed their portion by multiplying that tax rate times the value of their land and any improvements as assessed by government appraisers. The owner, or commonly their mortgage company through escrow, then pays periodically, whether quarterly, semi-annually, or otherwise set by law. Real estate investment loans often do not have escrow, so the owner there will be responsible for making the payments just like an owner who has no mortgage. Also, if an owner owns their property free and clear of any mortgages, they are still responsible for paying their property taxes.

If a given property owner does not pay the tax for their property by the government deadline, they are normally charged interest and penalties until they do. Until then, any past-due tax amount plus interest and penalties normally becomes a lien on the property, including improvements. This happens by operation of law and must be paid before the property can be sold. That tax lien normally moves into first position by law, meaning it jumps in front of any mortgage, mechanic's lien, HOA lien, heirs, etc., to be paid off first through the proceeds of any sale or foreclosure.

The problem for the government with this process is that unpaid tax liens just sitting around mean the locality's cash flow and budget are disrupted by the missing stack of money, potentially for years at a time. So, what is the government to do to get the cash it needs to meet immediate payroll and other obligations? Some localities have laws that allow them to foreclose on the property in a way very similar to a bank whose mortgage has not been paid. The jurisdiction gets the first batch of proceeds over costs from the tax foreclosure with any remainder typically going to mortgage holders, other lien holders, and any after that to the owner of record or heirs.

As you can imagine, local governments and politicians are not necessarily thrilled about foreclosing on citizens who vote and have friends and family who do as well. Plus, local governments are not normally sitting around with enough or the right kind of staff to handle the foreclosure process, which in any event can generate still more cash outflows before the taxes are ultimately collected. Some governments deal with this by just letting the tax lien sit indefinitely until the property is sold someday or a safety problem with the property arises.

Tax lien sales and auctions are the best answer to most of these problems from the government's perspective. The locality bundles up the past due taxes, penalties, and interest on a given property and sells that single tax lien in the form of a tax lien certificate to a private party based on a statutory or regulatory process. The government is happy because it immediately gets cash in hand to fund its budget, and the private party (in that party's name) must deal with any foreclosure or other effort to recoup the back taxes it bought. The private buyer of the tax lien has a variety of ways to get their tax lien investment paid off with interest (more on how that rate is set later), which again is normally written in a statute and interpreted by case law.

The details of the process to buy a tax lien and then recoup that investment as well as the calculation of interest earned, vary widely even among jurisdictions in the same state, and even among jurisdictions right next to each other. This is both fortunate and unfortunate. I say unfortunate because I cannot just lay out one standard rule for you to absorb. I say fortunate because the relative complexity and variations create a barrier to entry for anyone competing with you to learn about and buy the tax lien in each location. The investment of our time and effort in learning a handful of jurisdictions has made us a lot of money.

I will use Washington, DC, as an example here because it is one jurisdiction we know well and that has features like many others. You can often easily find the basic tax sale statute or code for most jurisdictions by a simple online search for tax lien sale or auction rules for the specific county or locality you are interested in learning. Some places like DC will even have in-person seminars or online guides that summarize their process. However, as you will see as we discuss the DC example, be very careful to *really* understand the nuances and pitfalls of any given jurisdiction that might not be obvious from just reading the controlling statute.

Talking to an attorney familiar with that jurisdiction *before* you buy a tax lien is a very good idea. Even though Ed is an attorney, this is the first thing he did. He sought out one of the few attorneys who knew the business well to get some of the nuances the statutes and key cases might not reveal. The attorney was generous with his time and we still use him to this day to handle our tax lien suits in DC.

You'll always want to learn the basics yourself first to keep costs down, but paying for insights on some of the nuances and pitfalls to watch out for before you buy will be money well spent. Registration, deposit, and winning auction payment requirements can be varied and detailed for each jurisdiction, but not typically that confusing, so we will not cover them in this book. As with all the other tax lien rules, read, and comply carefully! You've gotten this far, that part of the process should be easy for you.

DC typically conducts tax lien auctions every year in July. Months in advance, government staff identify properties with past due amounts over a certain threshold, meaning that years and big balances of past due taxes and penalties might have accrued until getting added to the auction list. Past-due letters and tax lien auction warnings are required by law and go out repeatedly to the owner(s) of record, some of whom pay. The others, who do not pay, go on the tax lien auction list that DC puts out to the public by late June or early July.

The DC auction list shows the square and lot number identifying each real estate parcel for tax purposes, along with the owner of record, any secondary owner, whether the property is improved or not, the street number (if any), street name, quadrant of DC, and the dollar amount of the tax lien being auctioned. The list is often more than 2,000 properties long. On pre-determined and announced days, each property lien (not the property itself) is auctioned off one by one going down the list by a live auctioneer in the DC tax offices. Some jurisdictions, such as Baltimore, use sealed bids submitted through the Internet, but that is not nearly as much fun.

So, you just pick a tax lien amount you can afford, buy the tax lien, and collect 18 percent (the statutory rate in DC)? No, it is not that simple, and randomly picking a property is like playing hopscotch in a minefield. You need to research to safely pick a property before you buy its lien, and you need to register and have the right amount of funds on hand to bid and be ready to close quickly on the purchase.

The number one thing you must look for in buying a tax lien is that the value of the property as it sits there (or with needed renovations) is sufficiently more than the amount of the tax lien and additional taxes that could accrue going forward. The reason the tax-to-valuation comparison is so important is that a property owner might simply fail to ever pay the taxes. At a certain point after about two to three years, (as we'll discuss later) you'll get title to the property *instead* of your tax lien investment and then you also become responsible for paying all the taxes that accrued since you bought the lien. (The time to get the property varies by jurisdiction; with Baltimore more like a year or so).

This getting-the-property-prize can be a fantastic result if the value of the property as it sits plus any required repairs substantially exceeds the total taxes. When this happens, you effectively get a fix-and-flip property to sell as is, repair and sell, keep as a rental, or whatever you like. However, if the tax lien plus additional tax exceeds the value of the property this is called losing. You get nothing, to quote Willy Wonka. That means no interest earnings, no (or partial) return of principal if the property is even salable, nothing other than a piece of property you will have little choice but to abandon or sell at a loss. No doubt at this point in the book you understand this result is bad and the opposite of a good real estate investment. The good news is, if you handle this evaluation correctly, you will have a tax lien earning significant interest that is extremely well protected by a tangible asset.

Let's dig down into how to research properties on a tax auction list, and then walk through the auction process, learning as we go. In DC, like most good-sized jurisdictions, a lot of property information is available free online. You would go to DC's real property assessment webpage and type in a search box the square and lot of a given property from the auction list. A lot of information pops up, based on which you can quickly delete some prospects from your list and further consider others.

Sample 1: A property from a recent DC auction list is square and lot 5175-0085. When I pulled up that assessment, it showed 1014 50th Street, NE, owned by MM&G Inc., which matches the info on the list. I see this has a DC use code of 12. This means residential; you can search online for DC use codes for more details. This is all very good so far. Perhaps it's an investment fix-and-flip gone wrong? There was a big tax lien for sale, a bit over $260,000 on the list. Don't worry, there are plenty in the range of a few thousand dollars, but big ones like this are great if you have the cash to invest because there is less competition to buy it (and thus drive down your interest return) and less effort than managing dozens of smaller liens to reach this amount. A quick look on Google Street View shows a dilapidated but okay one-story single-family home.

Sounds good? RUN AWAY! The same tax website also shows the assessed value as just about $200,000. Sometimes these assessments can be off for many reasons, but not normally by that much because DC reassesses annually. (Maryland normally reassesses every three years as a different example). If I bought this tax lien for about $260,000, nobody is going to pay off the taxes to get a $200,000 home even if they could, meaning I would owe subsequent taxes and get the property after a multi-year delay. Let's say I could sell it for $150,000 as is (because it needs $50,000 in repairs), I would lose more than $110,000. DC would be very happy.

Sample 2: Another high tax lien sample was 6095-0038, which is 3765 1st Street SE. It shows use 89, which typically means a church or special use, a tax lien price of about $152,000, and ownership by Deutsche Bank Trust Company. The assessed value is $1 million, and Google Street View shows a big lot so overgrown with weeds and trees I need to look at the overhead satellite picture to see if there is a large structure on site. Before I put so much money at risk, I would drive by and eyeball the property or have a helper do so for me to send a picture, so I am confident in the rough value and possible renovation exposure.

Next, I look at the estimated taxes due the following year, which total around $20,000–what I call the burn rate. In other words, I effectively will burn about $40,000 above the tax lien to hold this lean long enough for a two-year process to foreclose on the property or $50,000 for three years. In two years, I will have invested and must pay $152,000 plus $20,000 plus $20,000–or roughly $200,000 to get the property in my name. Of course, this assumes the taxes are not ultimately paid, which always remains most likely, but in that case, I'd get my investment money back with interest.

This all seems good so far because my tax lien would be well protected. Deutsche Bank Trust should be more likely than most to wake up and pay the taxes at some point. There is every reason for them or someone with an ownership interest to sell the property and pay the taxes given the equity it holds. Also, this is not my problem. If they or an heir or another relevant party does not pay all the taxes currently, before my foreclosure is concluded in about two to three years, I get a property previously assessed at $1 million for around $200,000 to $220,000. Even assuming $200,000 in a total renovation I could profit $600,000. I am told this is known as a win. The odds of getting a property like this are probably 1 percent or less in my experience, but the booby prize is getting back all my money with a lot of interest. I'll gladly take a free lottery ticket to get a house cheaply while I earn a lot of interest as my backup investment.

Sample 3: A more normal, medium price range lien was 5087-0902 at 4244 Benning Avenue, NE, use 12, class 1, and a tax lien of about $8,500. With an assessed value of $350,000, a burn rate of about $3,000 a year, and a nice-looking street view picture, this property is an easy yes for me. I know my investment will be well protected and most likely paid off relatively soon, though it would be a much bigger win were it not.

Auction Day

On auction day, the auctioneer very quickly works down through the one or two thousand properties like these by announcing square, lot, and address one at a time. Registered bidders have a card with their bidder ID number on it. Bids start at the exact total tax lien price listed. Sample 1 would start at the exact tax lien amount of $260,000 and the bidding only would go up for how much surplus to deposit with DC in addition to and over the tax lien amount. With only one bidder, the lien would go for $260,000. With multiple bidders, if it ended at say $10,000, the winner would have to pay $270,000 to DC.

However, presumably, nobody would bid on Sample 1 and DC would be stuck not getting its taxes paid. Periodically, DC will have a sale to auction off tax liens on underwater properties like this by taking bids starting at $1 on how much of the taxes to pay. In other words, in such an auction, I might bid up to something like $50,000 of the $260,000 to lien. The owner would still have to pay the full $260,000 plus accrued taxes to get the property while I would only effectively pay $50,000 plus accrued interest plus my attorney's fees and costs. This means I must bid the right amount going in knowing that I am likely to get (and pay) for the property.

Let's say I checked out Sample 2 and there indeed is a large building on a totally overgrown lot that looks like a complete gut renovation that could cost as much as $250,000. Assuming I am the only bidder, I will have to pay $152,000 to DC within five days or forfeit my deposit. I will earn the statutory 18 percent rate on $152,000 unless and until the taxes are paid. My attorney will handle the limited effort required to monitor and sue if needed–incurring sums that must be paid by the record holder with the back taxes to redeem the property. This is a rather nice passive income!

Sample 3 would be liked by many bidders. Whatever is paid to DC should be very well protected, and unlikely to result in the bidder getting the property (a hassle for some primarily interested in only the interest). Let's say that the winning bid is $25,000. What does that mean? This means the winner will pay DC the $8,500 for the tax lien plus $25,000 in what is known as a surplus, for a total payment of $33,500. Only the $8,500 earns interest for the winning bidder while DC gets to hold on to the $25,000 interest-free.

Why would anyone do this? This would still not be a bad rate of return when highly protected Treasury bills were still earning 2 percent and certificates of deposit under 1 percent. You can calculate the rate of return as follows: $8,500 tax lien / ($8,500 tax lien + $25,000 surplus) X 0.18 statutory interest = 4.56 percent. This is set for the life of the lien and does not go up or down regardless of market conditions. In other words, about a quarter of the money paid to DC earns 18 percent interest which can be expressed as an overall interest rate of 4.56 percent.

Let's say the winning bid instead was $15,000. This would be $8,500 tax lien / ($8,500 tax lien + $15,000 surplus) x 0.18 statutory interest = 6.51 percent. You simply need to decide in advance what rate of return you think is worth it for your money for two or three years (though redemption is more common within the first year) and stop bidding before you pass your minimum target. Plus, while you are holding that lottery ticket, I mean lien, don't forget that in around 1 percent of the cases you get the property for a return well above 18 percent if you've selected the target properly.

One nuance in DC, because the foreclosure process takes so long, is that the tax lien purchaser can buy those subsequently accruing taxes every six months or so, commonly referred to as "subsequents." The nice thing about this is that the price is equal to the taxes with no surplus markup, meaning that you get the full 18 percent of the subsequent purchase amount paid to DC. It also can be wise to buy the subsequents in case you get the property. Otherwise, to get the property, you would have to pay the subsequent taxes plus 18 percent interest to DC. Your cost of funds would probably be a lot lower to pay off the taxes as you go and earn the 18 percent if the owner pays.

Now that you own some tax liens, what the heck do you do next? There is a small group of competent lawyers who fully understand and handle DC tax liens and related land-use matters. You need to hire one (and would be wise to start the relationship before your first auction). In DC, you and your attorney must wait six months before filing a foreclosure action, but if you wait more than one year the tax lien is waived completely! Many tax lien holders who are happy with their interest rate will wait until closer to the one-year mark to sue for foreclosure, thinking that an owner who gets sued is more likely to act to bring their taxes current (including by selling the property), thereby ending their interest earnings.

The DC statute identifies the list of people who must be named as defendants in a tax lien foreclosure complaint. This includes record owners, as well as known heirs, but also lien holders such as banks, the District of Columbia, and others. An initial status conference will be set by the court roughly three to six months after the suit is filed.

No judgment of foreclosure can be entered until one year has passed from that first status conference or four months after the last party is served – whichever is later. Some cases can present difficult issues serving all the right parties. Sometimes, the parties sued will beg the judge for additional time to pay off the taxes and make all sorts of claims about their ability to raise money that often fail. The judge has a lot of discretion whether to grant an extension, and they often will do so.

Other unexpected issues can and will arise, and a tax case in DC easily could go three years or more from when the tax lien was purchased, depending on the original filing date, other unique circumstances related to the property and owners, and the judge. Keep this in mind when evaluating whether there is enough equity in the property to protect you! Owners can file bankruptcy or heirs can seek to open probate, and parties can dispute aspects of the proceeding in ways that can delay getting a judgment of foreclosure. In Minnesota, a party sued all the way to the Supreme Court, receiving a judgment in 2023 that the process used there was an unconstitutional taking as compared to other state procedures that were discussed as being just fine. Lengthy delays beyond two or three years generally are outliers in DC, and we've managed around them, but these are some of the nuances to consider that an experienced DC tax lien attorney can discuss with you.

Ultimately, the court will enter a judgment of foreclosure if the taxes are not redeemed in time. A process then ensues for DC to issue a foreclosure deed to the tax lien owner (you) who sued (or to whom the lien was assigned). This involves the payment to DC of any taxes incurred after the tax lien by the tax lien holder. The tax foreclosure deed wipes out almost any lien such as mortgages, HOA fees, etc., and is generally regarded for title insurance and other reasons to be of the best reliability. I say generally because certain government liens like those incurred for water use and recorded can still be owed by the tax lien purchaser. Any surplus that was paid to get the tax lien will be returned (or can be used to the extent needed to pay off the additional accrued taxes). All of this is a very manageable process, but again warrants help from a good attorney. Of note: The lien holder normally bears the statutorily allowed attorneys' fees incurred from the start of the process through redemption but the tax lien purchaser bears all fees and costs if issued a foreclosure deed.

As usual, there are nuances in DC and other jurisdictions as well. Properties in DC that are owner-occupied or heir-occupied as of the foreclosure suit filing do not go to the tax lien purchaser. Instead, DC amended its lien statute a few years ago to require that such properties must be auctioned. The tax lien holder then gets back their attorneys' fees and surplus and all the taxes they paid with 18 percent interest plus 10 percent if the proceeds are enough. Any amount above that goes to the owner or heir. The devil is in the details of this process, but the statute explains it in relatively plain terms and experienced DC lawyers can tell you all about it.

Another issue can be getting title insurance when reselling a property that you do obtain by foreclosure deed. Some title insurers can be gun-shy about the perceived risk of a prior owner or heir showing up late and trying to challenge the foreclosure deed after the property is resold to a third party. Enough title insurers realize this is not a significant concern, but it is another complexity and delay in cashing out that you might face. We have never had trouble getting normal title insurance after a bit of effort, but again, it's something to consider.

Redemption of the property by the record owner (or relevant party like a bank or an estate or heir) is possible at any time before a judgment of foreclosure. This entails payment to DC for all past due taxes, all interest incurred on the past due taxes, and all penalties. If this happens after a suit is filed, the redeeming party must contact the tax lien attorney to obtain a payoff amount for statutorily allowed fees and costs that were incurred. These too must be paid before redemption is complete.

After such a redemption, DC will turn around and pay the tax lien holder back with 18 percent interest on the tax lien amount. DC also will pay back any surplus but with no interest on that amount. As might already be clear, there is no compounding of interest and no return of the lien amount or interest until after redemption. Once the interest is paid, that becomes a distribution for which DC will issue a 1098 for the tax year in which the payment is made. If you have structured the retention of the attorney correctly, all or most of the attorneys' fees and costs ultimately will be covered by the redeeming party so the interest should be all profit to the tax lien purchaser.

Key Takeaways:

- High-interest earnings: Tax lien investing can generate significant returns, with interest rates potentially as high as 18 percent or 21 percent, depending on jurisdiction. These returns are relatively passive and well-protected but not without pitfalls.
- Lien priority: Tax liens typically take precedence over other types of liens, including mortgages and HOA liens. This puts tax lien investors in a strong position to recoup their investment plus interest.
- Jurisdiction matters: The process and laws governing tax liens vary widely, even among jurisdictions within the same state. Each jurisdiction has its own set of rules and nuances that investors need to understand to navigate the investment process successfully.
- Importance of Research: Before investing, it's crucial to research the value of the property attached to the tax lien. The property's value should significantly exceed the amount of the tax lien and any additional taxes that may accrue in the future.
- Legal consultation: Given the complexity and variations in laws, talking to an attorney who specializes in this area is highly

recommended. They can provide insights into local statutes and potential pitfalls that may not be obvious.

- Potential outcomes: If the property owner fails to pay back the tax lien amount within a set period (which varies by jurisdiction), the tax lien holder may eventually take ownership of the property. This can be lucrative if handled correctly but can result in a loss if the total taxes exceed the property's value.

Chapter 15

POOLED HARD MONEY MORTGAGE FUNDS

"Somebody said to me, 'But the Beatles were anti-materialistic.' That's a huge myth. John and I literally used to sit down and say, 'Now, let's write a swimming pool.'"
—Paul McCartney

Pooled mortgage funds are a type of investment vehicle that allows multiple investors to group their money together to invest jointly in issuing mortgages or real estate loans. These funds provide investors with access to a diverse portfolio of mortgage loans, which can offer higher returns than traditional investments such as stocks and bonds. One way that pooled mortgage funds can generate high returns is by engaging in the sort of hard money lending we've already discussed, which allows the fund to earn high-interest fees and costs in return for lending to borrowers who may not be able to qualify for less expensive traditional bank loans.

Pooled mortgage funds therefore can use hard money lending to generate high returns for their investors by lending to borrowers who may not be able to qualify for traditional bank loans. By taking on higher-risk borrowers, these funds can offer higher interest rates to their investors. However, this type of lending also comes with higher risks, as the borrowers may default on their loans, leading to losses for the fund and its investors. This sort of risk can be spread by having numerous hard money loans and multiple investors so that losses are more likely to be offset on average by more significant gains.

The fund management is going to need to make sure that they have complied with all of the regulatory requirements of managing and operating a fund before taking investment funds. Issuing shares for money or taking promissory notes for loans into a pooled fund can be considered an issuance of securities under the Securities Act of 1933, triggering costly regulatory and reporting requirements like those that apply to public stocks.

One way that pooled mortgage funds can minimize and streamline these registration requirements is by applying for Regulation D (known as Reg D) exemptions, such as 506B and 506C, to offer their pooled fund only to accredited investors. Such investors must be able to certify at least $1 million in net worth alone or with a spouse excluding their primary residence and/or at least $200,000 in annual income or $300,000 jointly. The Securities and Exchange Commission (SEC) created these criteria as a way to ensure that investors have the financial sophistication and resources to understand and assume the risks associated with certain types of investments. This includes private placements, hedge funds, venture capital funds, and other investments that are not registered with the SEC or subject to the same level of regulation as public offerings. By limiting these types of investment opportunities to accredited investors, the SEC aims to protect investors from potential fraud and ensure that only those with the financial capacity and knowledge to bear the risks can participate.

The main difference between 506B and 506D exemptions under Regulation D is how the fund can market the offering and verify the accredited status of investors. A fund using 506B can offer an unlimited number of accredited investors and up to thirty-five non-accredited investors. However, the company cannot use solicitations or advertising to market the offering to the general public and must take reasonable steps to verify the accredited status of investors.

On the other hand, 506C allows a private fund to offer securities only to accredited investors and requires that the company verify the accredited status of investors using specified methods. However, 506C does allow for general solicitation and advertising to market the offering, as long as all investors ultimately are verified as accredited.

Both of these methods have disclosure requirements, such as the creation of a formal prospectus for the accredited investor to review in order to understand risks, fund management, and withdrawal limitations, among other terms. Nevertheless, the contents of a prospectus that satisfy 506B or 506C are far less complex, onerous, and costly than a full registration for a security under the Securities Act. At the same time, what is required should still be sufficient to allow a relatively more sophisticated accredited investor to understand and accept or reject the risk that joining the fund would involve.

Pooled mortgage funds can provide investors with access to a diverse portfolio of mortgage loans, which can offer higher returns than traditional investments. Hard money lending can be a useful tool for these funds to generate high returns by lending to borrowers who may not be able to qualify for traditional bank loans. However, these funds also come with higher risks, and using Reg D exemptions and other regulatory frameworks can help provide greater transparency and oversight for investors.

Fund management is a key element associated with the operation of a 506B hard money fund. The fund manager is responsible for overseeing the fund's investments and operations and may charge a management fee, which is typically a percentage of the fund's assets under management. The manager may also charge a performance fee, which is based on the fund's returns. Overall, the fund manager needs to have the necessary skills and experience to effectively manage the fund and generate returns for investors. The required prospectus should include this information.

The 506B fund Clear Sky put together was a debt offering. We offered investors a fixed return on their investment. If you put in $1 million and we were paying a 7.5 percent return, you could count on us paying you $6,250 a month in interest payments. Your investment was then spread across our entire hard money portfolio, so if one loan did not perform, you didn't get a reduced payment. This also created an incentive for us to make as good decisions as possible with your investment since we only earn money if we generate returns over the 7.5 percent cost of funds.

Fund governance is another important element to consider. The fund must have a governing document, such as a limited partnership agreement or operating agreement, which outlines the rights and responsibilities of the fund's investors and managers. The governing document also specifies how profits and losses are allocated among the investors. It's important for the fund manager to have a clear understanding of the governing document and to ensure that it is being followed in the operation of the fund. Unfortunately, there is a balance between legal disclosure and clarity of thought. At the most basic level, we offered a 7.5 percent return on your million-dollar investment, as we discussed. When it came to signing the disclosure documents, you faced nearly a hundred pages of legal disclosures.

Investor reporting is another key element associated with the operation of a 506B hard money fund. The fund is required to provide regular reports to its investors, which typically include financial statements and updates on the fund's performance and investments. The fund must also comply with all SEC reporting requirements and provide investors with certain disclosures, such as risks associated with the fund's investments. The fund manager needs to provide regular and transparent reporting to investors, as this helps to build trust and maintain strong relationships.

The formation and operation of a 506B hard money fund involve several key elements, including establishing a legal entity, identifying qualified accredited investors, developing an investment strategy, managing the fund's investments and operations, adhering to a governing document, providing regular investor reporting, and complying with all applicable securities laws and regulations. It's important for the fund manager to have a clear understanding of each of these elements and to work closely with investors to build a successful fund that generates strong returns.

Operating the fund and filling it with performing assets is another book entirely. A hard money fund manager spends a lot of time managing risk before a loan is given, and even more time tracking the fund's loans and collecting from delinquent borrowers. We have found that this is a great line of business as a diversification from direct real estate investment. However, you need to have plenty of capital and time to get a fund going. The first step to investing in or properly running a hard money fund is to understand the assets in your portfolio, as described in this book!

Key Takeaways:

- Pooled mortgage funds: These funds allow investors to pool money for issuing real estate loans, offering diversification, and potentially higher returns.
- Regulatory compliance: Funds must adhere to laws such as the Securities Act of 1933 to operate legally.
- Regulation D exemptions: 506B and 506C exemptions streamline compliance by targeting accredited investors.
- Fund management: Effective management is critical for overseeing investments and generating returns.
- Fund governance: Proper governance, usually outlined in a legal document, is essential for operational clarity and fairness.
- Investor reporting: Regular, transparent reporting builds investor trust and fulfills legal requirements.

WELCOME TO YOUR DESTINATION

"F*** YOU MONEY"

Jim Bennett: I've been up two and a half million dollars [from gambling].
Frank: What you got on you?
Jim Bennett: Nothing.
Frank: What you put away?
Jim Bennett: Nothing.
*Frank: You get up two and a half million dollars, any as***** in the world knows what to do. You get a house with a twenty-five-year roof, an indestructible . . . shitbox, you put the rest into the system at three to five percent to pay your taxes and that's your base, get me? That's your fortress of f****** solitude. That puts you, for the rest of your life, at a level of f*** you. Somebody wants you to do something, f*** you. Boss pisses you off, f*** you! Own your house. Have a couple bucks in the bank. Don't drink. That's all I have to say to anybody on any social level. Did your grandfather take risks?*
Jim Bennett: Yes.
*Frank: I guarantee he did it from a position of f*** you. A wise man's life is based around f*** you. The United States of America is based on f*** you. You're a king? You have an army? Greatest navy in the history of the world? F*** you!*

—Mark Wahlberg and John Goodman in The Gambler

We promised at the start of this book to provide you with a roadmap to wealth through real estate investing. We want you to enjoy every mile and waypoint along your trip as much as we have ours. Done right, you will meet and work with a lot of interesting people, have fun putting together winning real estate deals, and learn and improve a lot about yourself. If you are not having a lot of fun along the way, in between a few unpleasant potholes, you might want to consider a course correction. We have had a blast every step of the way and we continue to invest in real estate because we still laugh and have fun with the process while working together and making money.

One of the best parts of our journey that we are most proud of is the number of millionaires we have helped create over the years by sharing our real estate investing experience. Our insights and principles, combined of course with their enormous dedication and hard work, have helped create 7 millionaires — the Tiens, Jads, Armandos, Joels, Omars, Ace/Akams, and Latorres.

They all are great people whose success brings a smile to our faces, but one story in particular stands out, investor Harold Latorre. Harold came to us in early 2021 to borrow money for fix and flips. He did not have any fix and flip experience and was considered a Level 1 investor. We love meeting Level 1 investors because we believe that with our help and guidance at the start of their path, we can help guide them to Level 5.

Harold started out as a handyman working for another company. He did not know us personally, and instead got our names through one of our online marketing efforts. He went to a couple of local real estate meet-up groups to learn more about us and using other people's money to fund fix and flips. Harold asked around and found many who gave us great reviews, the best kind of word-of-mouth advertising.

Harold has borrowed money for twelve fix-and-flip deals in the two and a half years from meeting us to our writing of this book. He made a great average profit of about $70,000 per deal. Maybe you're thinking, *that only equals $840,000, this isn't millionaire status.* But wait, there's more. Harold used his profits as a down payment on buy-and-hold investment properties and currently owns ten cash-producing rentals. Market appreciation has pushed him and his rentals over a $1 million net worth.

Our other millionaire investors have used us in many ways, like helping them find the assets, helping them find the money (even though it might not have been via our hard money loans), or helping in their real estate investing education. Many have started at the very beginning when they've known little or nothing about real estate. They wanted to learn from the start about how to wholesale and how to fix and flip. We also have had other investors who already had some experience in other areas of investing, they had a pretty decent background behind them and they entered our program somewhere in the middle.

The point is we know for a fact you can have this same level of success from whatever level you start as long as you put in the same sort of effort. We have given you every bit of information we could fit in here just so that you will be able to move forward into real estate with confidence from wherever you start. This book has given you a better understanding of where you sit now, which in turn will help you understand where you can jump in and what education you still need. You can really start from anywhere.

But you do need to start. The number one way to fail is a failure to act. This is how most people lose before they even start the journey. They see where others are and tell themselves that achieving success such as that is impossible without a pile of cash to start. Remember paralysis by analysis? Do not, however, try to do everything at once. This will end badly. You cannot overwhelm yourself and try to speed up the process of learning. Pick one thing and finish it, then move on to the next thing until you have completed your checklist. Trust the process – you now know it works!

Once you turn the last page in this book, take that momentum and find a seminar you can attend. Continue this cycle of momentum building by starting with the simple action items in this book. This will help you find the right start for yourself on the roadmap, and in turn, give you much more confidence to be able to suss out which option is best for you and your situation. If you still have questions or want to explore any of the many areas we covered in greater depth, head on over to our website,www.realestateroadmaptowealth.com. We have a lot of tools and tidbits waiting for you there and much more on the way.

But one last question still remains; how do *you* know when *you* have reached *your* destination on our roadmap? In other words, what does it really mean to be wealthy? We can tell you what it has meant to us and perhaps this will resonate with you. To us, being wealthy means having enough money to get what we and our families need and the financial freedom to do what we want when we want to do it. We can say no to anyone and anything and yes if and when that is what we want to do. Perhaps even more importantly, wealth means having the time and resources to spend and share with our loved ones and give back to our communities.

We want you to walk away from reading this book with a real understanding of what it really means to be financially independent. At its core, financial independence is far from a mere numerical equation; it's a profound paradigm shift. It's about achieving a delicate equilibrium where the scale tips in your favor, where your passive income, those streams of revenue that flow into your coffers without you actively toiling for each dollar, stand tall and confident, matching or surpassing the sum total of your monthly expenses. It's the sweet spot where you're no longer a hostage to your bills, but rather the conductor of your life's symphony.

So the real journey you are now on is rewriting the script of your life. It's about reclaiming the hours you'd otherwise spend tethered to your nine-to-five grind and investing them in pursuits that set your soul ablaze. It's about having the freedom to explore, experiment, and engage with the world on your terms, unshackled by the chains of monetary obligations. You are at your destination when you are free.

ABOUT THE AUTHORS

Charlie Einsmann started as an internet tech guy in Herndon,Virginia before he figured out how to find and buy his first distressed property with little but credit cards. Charlie soon walked out of his cubicle for the last time with his buddy Sam to co-create and co-own the Clear Sky Group to develop hundreds of fix and flips, build a massive rental portfolio, and lend tens of millions of dollars through their private pooled mortgage fund.

Sam Jacknin sat a few cubicles over as a client services rep when he started studying to get his real estate broker's license. Sam quickly partnered with Charlie to co-create and co-own the Clear Sky Group to efficiently find, buy, repair, and sell distressed properties, manage an ever-growing rental portfolio, and run their huge pooled mortgage fund.

Ed Grass came along a little later, after being a litigation partner at a top 25 law firm when limb-girdle muscular dystrophy made it impossible to continue. Ed had saved some money along the way, so he started investing with Sam and Charlie to keep busy, and ultimately became their go-to guy to dream up the next big idea and navigate the most unusual legal issues.

Made in the USA
Columbia, SC
11 April 2024

34213971R00130